MEDITERRANEAN DIET
RECIPES&PREPARATION

Saskia Fraser is a healthy-foods expert, author and lifestyle coach. She has helped thousands of busy working women to experience greater energy, mental clarity and self-confidence. Saskia runs raw-food detox courses and workshops, in person and online, as well as one-to-one life-coaching programmes. She is the author of *Raw Freedom*, a raw-food recipe book for busy lives, as well as a popular raw-food blog and three other books for Flame Tree: *Superfoods, Raw Food* and *Vegan Food*.

Publisher & Creative Director: Nick Wells
Senior Project Editor: Catherine Taylor
Copy Editor: Adèle Linderholm
Art Director: Mike Spender
Layout Design: Jane Ashley
Digital Design & Production: Chris Herbert

Special thanks to Dawn Laker, Olivia Jermy, Rachel Greiner, Frances Bodiam.

FLAME TREE PUBLISHING
6 Melbray Mews, Fulham,
London SW6 3NS, United Kingdom
www.flametreepublishing.com

First published 2019

Copyright © 2019 Flame Tree Publishing Ltd

21 23 22 20
3 5 7 9 10 8 6 4 2

ISBN: 978-1-78755-771-0

Printed in China

Images: © StockFood and the following: 68, 91 Erricson, Colin; 86 adolforuizmaeso; 100 hlphoto; 154 PhotoCuisine / Aubergine Studio; 157 Kia, Nu; 159 Great Stock!; 165 PhotoCuisine / A Point Studio; 166 Morgans, Gareth; 168 Hilden Smith, Eva; 173 Sporrer/Skowronek; 174 Richard Jackson Photography; 180 Paul, Michael ; 186 Thomas, Karen; 189 Parissi, Lucy; 199 Gräfe & Unzer Verlag / Kramp + Gölling; 201 Garlick, Ian; 206 Gräfe & Unzer Verlag / Schardt, Wolfgang; 208 Studio Lipov; 213 Hendey, Magdalena; 218 Brooks-Dammann, Susan; 221 Strokin, Yelena. © Shutterstock and the following: 7bl Elijah Lovkoff; 9b, 28-29, 123 Foxys Forest Manufacture; 6bl Ailynn; 9t Olesya Kuznetsova; 6br, 25br mythja; 7br brodtcast; 13b Losangela; 13t Vulcano; 14bl Andy Wasley; 224 Lukaszimilena; 4 Julia Suditskaya; 1, 14br Nadianb; 48-49 Cara-Foto; 14, 64 Elena Eryomenko; 17tl Marian Weyo; 17b Pawel Kazmierczak; 17tr Sebastian Duda; 19t Jack Frog; 19br Pazargic Liviu; 19bl Ilaszlo; 20t marilyn barbone; 20b Anastasiia Malinich; 22bl lightwavemedia; 22b4, 95, 113 zi3000; 23bl Wild As Light; 23br Kerdkanno; 25t ALEXEY IZOTOV; 25bl Mikhail_Kayl; 26t Yuganov Konstantin; 26b Jet Cat Studio; 30t Alicja Nuemiler; 30b 5PH; 33t Valerio Pardi; 33b Ziashusha; 34t Maria Uspenskaya; 34b Okrasyuk; 37t, 108 Ekaterina Kondratova; 37b Leonid Ikan; 38tl freedomnaruk; 38br Melica; 38tr Izalan Somai; 38bl Sea Wave; 41t stockcreations; 41br Nitr; 41bl Alexander Rutz; 43bl New Africa; 42bl Nito; 42br Ryzhkov Photohraphy; 45t vsl; 43br Magdanatka; 45b Pronina Marina; 46t Valeria Aksakova; 46bl, 117 Irina Rostokina; 46br Lukas Gojda; 51tl Marco Mayer; 51tr Tapui; 52t sabrisy; 55t eugenegurkov; 55b Africa Studio; 57t Billion Photos; 58bl kazoka; 57b Daxiao Productions; 58br Dean Drobot; 59bl Catalin Petolea; 59br Odua Images; 3 Inna Luzan; 61t Minerva Studio; 52b Stokkete; 61b Yulia Grigoryeva; 67 Pinkyone; 71 Irina Goleva; 72, 77, 89, 147 Kiian Oksana; 75, 185 MariaKovaleva; 78 Karissaa; 82, 139 AnjelikaGr; 85, 106 Anna_Pustynnikova; 92, 130 Albina Bugarcheva; 97 Anna Shepulova; 105 nesavinov; 111 Lapina Maria; 115, 153, 195 hlphoto; 121 topotishka; 124, 127, 190, 193 Barbara Dudzinska; 128 Slawomir Fajer; 133 Gayane; 134 supercat; 141 comeirrez; 143 Liliya Kandrashevich; 145, 196 Elena Trukhina; 149 Bartosz Luczak; 161 cobraphotography; 163 Magnago; 177 LongJon; 205 Rosalie.S.Photo; 214 thefoodphotographer; 217 usmee; and small watercolour illustrations throughout: Nadezhda Molkentin, Le Panda and Paket.

MEDITERRANEAN DIET
RECIPES&PREPARATION

Saskia Fraser

FLAME TREE
PUBLISHING

CONTENTS

Introduction   6

The Wonder Diet   10

Breakfast   62

Sides, Sauces & Dips   80

Soups & Light Meals   98

Mains: Salads & Vegetables   118

Mains: Fish & Seafood   150

Mains: Meat & Poultry   178

Treats & Desserts   202

Index   222

INTRODUCTION

WELCOME TO THE MEDITERRANEAN DIET!

The traditional Mediterranean diet has been hailed as one of the healthiest and most popular diets in the world and, in these pages, you will discover why. I will be introducing you to a diverse selection of delicious recipes to suit your health aspirations, budget and skills in the kitchen, whatever they may be. In this day and age eating a healthy diet is getting easier and easier. Good ingredients are available in most places and, with books like this, inspiration and motivation is close at hand.

When I am looking for new recipes, it is the natural beauty of the food that gets my creative juices flowing. Within these pages you will find plenty to inspire you. There

are breakfasts, sauces, sides, main meals, desserts and treats to tantalize your taste buds every day of the week, whether you are feeding the family, cooking dinner for one or entertaining at the weekend.

The Mediterranean diet has a tradition many thousands of years old, based on natural wholefoods available in the sunny climes of the countries bordering the Mediterranean Sea. Primarily when we speak of the Mediterranean diet, we are talking of the local, traditional diets of Italy, Greece and southern Spain and France. Many of the old recipes live on as traditions passed down from generation to generation, when produce would have been grown in people's back gardens, cheese would be made at home and fish would be caught fresh that day.

In the international world that we now live in, wherever we are we are lucky enough to be able to find the same produce used for thousands of years in the Mediterranean. Delicatessens and websites selling specialist ingredients are plentiful, while most of the fruits and vegetables of the Mediterranean are available

in our local stores. A variety of good-quality meat and fresh fish is easier to buy, and organic food and farmers' markets are becoming more plentiful. Eating healthily is now much more accessible.

What I personally love about the Mediterranean diet is that it allows you to eat some of the most delicious food in the world while still looking after your health. Simply by eliminating processed foods, reducing animal products, dairy and sugar, and increasing the amount of fresh fruit and vegetables you eat, you can dramatically improve your health, physically, mentally and emotionally.

Want more energy? Try the Mediterranean diet. Want to lose weight? Try the Mediterranean diet. Want to reduce the risk of disease? Try the Mediterranean diet. Some claim that eating the Mediterranean diet can even reverse illnesses such as heart disease and type 2 diabetes. Whatever the outcome you seek, the Mediterranean way of eating is a brilliant and tasty way to get closer to that goal.

Enjoy!

THE WONDER DiET

WHAT IS A MEDITERRANEAN DIET?

The Mediterranean Sea borders many beautiful countries with varied food cultures, from the coastlands of Spain, France and Italy, to the islands of Greece, the beaches of Turkey and the North African continent.

Mediterranean food is a celebration of the delicious produce grown and harvested in the region. The high quality of fresh ingredients has evolved into a culinary language of its own, where flavours shine through in a wide variety of dishes. Beautifully simple and healthy Mediterranean food can be produced in minutes at the end of the day, or slow cooked to produce rich and deeply satisfying meals for family and friends.

THE MEDITERRANEAN DIET

The Mediterranean diet is regarded as one of the healthiest diets in the world. Although the Mediterranean Sea borders countries in Europe, the Middle East and North Africa, the 'Mediterranean diet' mostly consists of classic dishes from southern France, Italy and Greece, with influences from Spain, Turkey and Morocco. The peoples of these regions have been known historically for their good health, eating diets high in fruits and vegetables, nuts, pulses, grains, fresh fish, sun-drenched herbs and spices, and of course plenty of olive oil.

The traditional Mediterranean diet contains a higher quantity of fresh fruits and vegetables, with less meat and fewer dairy foods than many other traditional diets. Dishes that are often thought of as 'vegetarian' are a normal part of the traditional culture, and a meal without meat or fish is not considered unusual. The region is also known for its fresh fish and meat dishes, used to wonderful effect in Mediterranean cooking.

COUNTRIES FULL OF FLAVOUR

The countries on the Mediterranean Sea have an abundance of fresh, dried and cured produce full of amazing flavour. With such good-quality produce, simple dishes with few ingredients can be created easily. Each province has its own unique style of flavours to tantalise your taste buds.

Italy

Most often when we envisage Mediterranean food, we are thinking of Italian and Greek food. Italian recipes tend to be characterised by natural sun-filled flavours, field-ripened fruits and vegetables, and fresh herbs such as rosemary and oregano. Protein is often a secondary consideration, where bold and rich flavours are combined in simple recipes.

When Italians eat meat, it is usually cured or cooked long and slowly, while quick-cooked seafood and fish are combined beautifully with fresh herbs. Pasta is of course synonymous with Italy and, in recent years, it has also become the leading producer of gluten-free pastas.

Greece

Greece and its islands are a bucket-list destination for many people, not only for its turquoise waters and white sand beaches but also for its world-renowned cuisine. On my first visit to Greece I was surprised by how many of their traditional recipes were naturally vegetarian. Greeks make no real distinction between dishes with or without meat or fish; to them it is all delicious, locally produced food.

They make most of their cheeses from goats' or sheep's milk. Feta and Halloumi are both traditionally made without cow dairy products, making them a healthier alternative to other cheeses.

France

French cuisine is famous throughout the world and has a long history of artisanal foods and recipes, varying from sophisticated city fare to countryside simplicity. The Mediterranean coast of France produces delicious recipes using outstanding fresh ingredients, with influences from Spain in the west and Italy in the east. All the ingredients one associates with France are in evidence, with garlic, wine, mustard and mixed herbs used in many of the traditional French Mediterranean dishes. The coastal influence is seen in the wide use of fresh and salted fish in recipes.

Spain

Although Spanish food in general is not considered particularly healthful, the southern coastal areas and islands of this beautiful country naturally produce an abundance of fresh ingredients. Specialising in seafood and fresh fish, recipes from this area often have a Moorish influence, incorporating grains and warming, smoky spices from North Africa.

Turkey

The roots of Turkish cuisine come from the Ottoman Empire. As with every part of the Mediterranean, the cuisine on the Turkish coast is influenced by neighbouring countries. It is generally lighter and healthier than recipes from other Turkish regions, with fresh vegetables, fish and herbs being predominant.

Morocco

The northernmost coast of Morocco verges on the Mediterranean. Its cuisine is quite different from that of other countries directly on the Mediterranean, with its main influences being Berber and Arabic. Recipes are apt to contain more spices and are often cooked long and slowly. Fewer dairy products are used, but plenty of fresh vegetables and dried fruits are included.

WHY EAT A MEDITERRANEAN DIET?

The traditional Mediterranean diet as we know it originally comes from Italy, Greece and the coastal regions of southern Spain and France, with influences from other countries around the Mediterranean Sea. Having evolved over thousands of years, it contains an abundance of wholefoods in the form of fresh vegetables, fruit, grains, pulses, nuts, seeds and fish.

The Mediterranean diet has become synonymous with 'the good life' while also being heralded as a lifestyle diet that promotes physical and emotional wellbeing due to its nutrient density. Certainly, in comparison to the modern Western diet, it is an incredibly healthy, fun and tasty way to eat. Children and adults alike enjoy the flavours and textures of this diet that has been eaten in the Mediterranean for millennia, with plant foods being the main foundation and plenty of health-promoting olive oil at almost every meal.

On the rough coastal lands of southern Europe, the dominant animals kept for milk were goats and sheep, producing a rich culture of cheese and yogurt made from these healthier milks. The slaughtering of an animal was a special occasion rather than the norm, meaning that meat was not the go-to source of protein but a treat. Eating less meat, we now know, is good for health on many levels.

THE HEALTH BENEFITS

The traditional Mediterranean diet developed over time into one of the healthiest diets in the world. As we learn more about nutrition and diet in this modern age, we are coming to appreciate the value and common sense of eating in this natural and simple way.

Many studies have been conducted into the health benefits of the Mediterranean diet. Evidence is growing that, along with exercise and reduced stress, it can increase life expectancy and reduce the risk of many diseases. It has even been proven to aid in reversing illnesses such as heart disease, diabetes and depression.

A high consumption of refined sugar, salt, grain and fat products, as well as low-quality meat and cow dairy, makes up most people's diets in the developed world. While many aspects of our lives have improved in the Western world, health is not one of them. Diet plays a large role in this decline in health and increase in disease.

Development means that we are also lucky to have an abundance of ingredients available to us, and as such we are able to take our health back into our own hands. By reclaiming traditional ways of eating, as with the Mediterranean diet, we can improve our mental, emotional and physical wellbeing far beyond what we thought possible.

High Fibre

With all the vegetables, fruit, pulses, legumes and grains in the Mediterranean diet, you naturally consume a large proportion of foods high in soluble and insoluble fibre. Consuming both types of fibre regularly in your diet is good for bowel health. A healthy bowel is essential for overall physical and emotional wellbeing. The gut has been dubbed 'the second brain' because of its importance. Dietary fibre also helps to control blood sugar levels, which is useful in avoiding type 2 diabetes and hypoglycaemia. Soluble fibre is said to aid in lowering cholesterol and to potentially lower blood pressure and inflammation.

Good Dairy

Many people are dairy intolerant without realising it. However, even for those with dairy intolerance, dairy products made from goats' and sheep's milk are often much easier to digest. Goats and sheep have one stomach as opposed to cows with four stomachs. This could explain why humans find it easier to digest goat and sheep dairy, as we also have only one stomach.

The consumption of dairy products has been linked to eczema and asthma as well as general inflammation in the body. The Mediterranean diet is naturally low in dairy products. Traditionally milk, cheese and yogurt would have been unpasteurised, which some people now believe to be better for you.

Less Meat

Although meat contains essential nutrients that can be hard to find in other foods, eating too much of it has been linked to the increase in modern inflammatory diseases including heart disease, cancer and digestive illnesses. Because the Mediterranean diet uses a higher proportion of plant-based foods, the ratio of animal to plant foods is naturally lower.

Although it is now well known that eating less meat is much better for our health, many people rely heavily on animal protein when it comes to cooking. If you struggle to know what to cook if not cooking with meat, the Mediterranean diet will give you many delicious recipes to try.

Nutrient Density

When you eat a Mediterranean diet, you are naturally eating a nutrient dense diet. Why is this important? Your body relies on the food you eat for cell regeneration, healing and cleansing. If the quality of the food you eat is inferior, your body has inferior building blocks to work with. When you eat a nutrient dense diet, your body is able to heal and regenerate much more effectively and efficiently, giving you more energy and a better sense of wellbeing, as well as aiding in the healing of illness. For maximum nutrient content, it is important to eat as much organic food as possible.

Healthy Fats

With all its olive oil, avocado, fish, nuts and seeds, the Mediterranean diet is incredibly rich in healthy fats. Olive oil is very high in a monounsaturated fat called oleic acid. The many studies into the health benefits of olive oil suggest that oleic acid aids in the reduction of inflammation, helping to reduce the risks of inflammatory diseases such as

cancer, heart disease, arthritis, autoimmune disease and asthma. Healthy fats can also help with weight loss. In the Mediterranean diet, replacing unhealthy fats with between two and four tablespoons of olive oil a day has been shown to potentially improve a number of health conditions.

Quality Produce

One of the characteristics of the Mediterranean diet is the quality of the ingredients. Quality is important when it comes to health because better-quality produce is more nutritious for us. Organic, sun-ripened, grass-fed, wild-caught and artisan are all bywords for quality. As well as tasting so much better and increasing the nutrient content of our meals, by choosing good-quality organic ingredients we are also reducing the quantity of chemicals we ingest and absorb through our food, which is crucial to wellbeing. Luckily, good-quality organic fresh produce, cheese, eggs and meat are becoming more readily available locally and online.

Red Wine

Drinking wine with meals has been part of the Mediterranean way of life for thousands of years. It has been reported that drinking a glass of wine, particularly red wine, a day can have health benefits. Wine is made from fermented grapes and therefore has a high vitamin and mineral content. It also contains antioxidants that boost the immune system and can help to protect against inflammation. The quality and quantity of the wine you consume is relevant to health. Many modern wines contain sulphites and additives, so choose organic wines. A small glass of wine a day may keep the doctor away, but if you want to be well drink in moderation.

FLAVOUR

When I think of Mediterranean food, I think of healthy food full of rich flavours and sunshine. Many people find it difficult to succeed with special diets because they

find them restrictive and boring. However, one of the main reasons the Mediterranean diet has become so successful and popular is because the food tastes so good. This interest in flavour has arisen from the wide range of ingredients available in these warm, sunny countries. Sun-ripened fresh produce, organic ingredients and a wide variety of seasonings are used to create sensational and healthy dishes.

Mediterraneans are masterful when it comes to their use of herbs such as basil, thyme and rosemary, spices such as paprika, nutmeg and saffron, and natural flavourings such as lemon, olives and capers. The Mediterranean way of eating is more of a lifestyle than a diet, so there is never any need to feel bored or restricted by your options. Although you may be learning to cook from scratch in order to follow it, the Mediterranean diet is incredibly diverse and delicious. It gives you the opportunity to learn how good you can feel when eating the right food.

YOUR BIG WHY

There are, unfortunately, no short cuts to good health. Taking care of your diet, and therefore your physical and emotional wellbeing, requires a level of commitment to the long-term outcome of your wellness. If you need motivation, look at people around you as they age and become more and more unwell. Look at how they eat. Health and diet tend to be very closely linked. If you wish to avoid the common diseases that our society is riddled with, start by taking care of your diet. Each shortcut that you habitually take – every ready-meal, fast-food snack or sugar pick-me-up – is likely to be reflected by your health in the long term.

Your number one place to start improving your health is through learning to cook nutritious and tasty breakfasts, lunches and dinners that you and your body love. When it comes to healthy eating, simplicity is key to success. Whether you are new to cooking or have been cooking from scratch for years, Mediterranean recipes are some of the easiest and tastiest to follow. Get in touch with what will motivate you most to eat healthily and to feel excited about learning these new recipes.

KEY FOODS

The abundantly healthy recipes that flourish around the Mediterranean focus on super-fresh ingredients and simple cooking methods. Simple is never boring when it comes to foods fresh from the ocean and fruits and vegetables grown under the sun. A good dish can be made delicious by using the best-quality ingredients.

Mediterranean-inspired fresh produce tastes wonderful as well as being good for you. Fruits and vegetables should be the staple element of a good diet, supporting overall wellness and helping to maintain a healthy weight. Many of your essential nutrients come from these foods, so it is important to buy organic whenever possible.

VEGETABLES

The Mediterranean diet contains some of the most delicious vegetables available. High in dietary fibre, they are the foundation of a healthy diet. Buying good-quality organic fresh produce will improve the taste of your food, as well as delivering more nutrients.

Aubergine (Eggplant)

Aubergines come in many different varieties. Some are bitter unless salted first. They are a good source of vitamins B1 and B6, potassium, copper, magnesium and manganese, as well as being high in antioxidants.

Avocado

Avocados have become a popular health food over recent years, and for good reason. They are a rich source of good fats, as well as folate, potassium and vitamins C, B5, B6 and E.

Red/Yellow/Green Pepper

Red, yellow and green peppers are packed full of antioxidants and are a very good source of vitamin C. They contain carotenoids, which have been linked to good vision as well as improving overall health.

Courgette (Zucchini)

Courgettes are a form of summer squash. They are high in antioxidants and anti-inflammatory phytonutrients, as well as being packed full of vitamins and minerals. Replacing grain pastas with courgette noodles can aid weight loss.

Onion

Onions come in a variety of types, including white onions, red onions and spring onions (scallions). They are low in calories while being high in nutrients, containing the antioxidant quercetin with its host of health benefits.

Salad Leaves

There are many different types of salad leaves in the Mediterranean diet, from lettuce to radicchio and rocket (arugula). High in water content, they are also satisfying due to their high nutrient content.

Spinach

Spinach is used widely throughout the Mediterranean, both in its raw and cooked form. High in iron, calcium and magnesium, it contains many essential minerals and vitamins that aid good physical and emotional health.

Tomato

Tomatoes are synonymous with the Mediterranean. Becoming sweet and juicy under the sun's rays, they are a source of the antioxidant lycopene whose many health benefits include a reduced risk of heart disease and cancer.

FRUIT

The high-water content and natural sugars found in fresh fruit are a source of natural energy. Be sure to smell fruit when buying – the sweet scent of natural ripeness means it is perfect for eating.

Grapefruit

White and pink grapefruits are slightly different in flavour, with pink grapefruits being sweeter. High in vitamins and minerals, grapefruit may aid in preventing diabetes.

Lemon

Lemons are widely used in the Mediterranean diet, lending their flavour to sweet and savoury dishes. Both the zest and juice contain health benefits.

Orange

Oranges are well known to be good for you. Just one medium orange a day is enough for your recommended daily amount of vitamin C.

Pomegranate

Pomegranates contain higher levels of antioxidants than most other fruit. Their health properties can be used to ease urinary tract infections, such as cystitis.

Fig

Figs are a good source of soluble fibre, making a satisfying snack. Introducing them into your diet can help with weight loss and relieve constipation.

Peach

Peaches are delicious cooked as well as raw. High in antioxidants, they contain vitamins and minerals that are particularly good for your skin and hair.

Apricot

Apricots contain vitamins A, C, E and K and niacin, as well as being a good source of trace minerals. Eat them fresh, cooked or dried.

HERBS & SPICES

Herbs and spices have been used in traditional medicine for thousands of years. They are an essential part of the Mediterranean diet, contributing flavour and goodness to recipes. Adding them to dishes is a tasty way to help boost health.

Garlic

Garlic has antibacterial and antifungal properties and is said to be good for heart health, as well as protecting against cancer. Use it raw in dressings or cooked in savoury dishes.

Oregano

Fresh or dried oregano, as well as oregano oil (used medicinally) has strong antimicrobial properties and can help improve gut health. Try it fresh in salads and with fish or dried in casseroles and pasta dishes.

Rosemary

Rosemary's pungent smell comes from a range of plant oils that are said to be antimicrobial, antifungal and anti-inflammatory. Add fresh rosemary to lamb dishes, and even to desserts.

Basil

Basil is a good source of vitamins A and K. It has antibacterial properties and may help with inflammatory ailments. It is most flavourful when eaten fresh and raw on salads or on top of savoury dishes.

Chili

Chilies contain capsaicin, a substance that is said to help relieve pain as well as inflammation. Stir it, fresh or dried, through pasta dishes and soups.

MEAT

Although one of the noticeable features of the Mediterranean diet is the inclusion of a high proportion of plant-based ingredients, meat also plays an important role. It provides essential nutrients that are hard to find in other foods, helping to build muscle and sustain energy.

Poultry

Chicken and turkey are lean meats that are good for heart health. High in protein, they contribute to muscle development and help to balance blood sugar when eaten as part of a balanced diet. It is important to cook poultry properly as raw chicken and turkey can harbour salmonella.

Lamb

Lamb is used in such classic dishes as Greek Moussaka and Moroccan Tagines. In Mediterranean recipes it is often cooked slowly, making it tender and flavoursome. High in essential B vitamins and minerals, lamb is a nutrient-dense food that is also a good source of iron.

Beef

Eating too much red meat is not necessarily good for health. However, beef is an amazing source of iron and its consumption can be useful in treating iron deficiency. As part of a balanced diet, beef contributes essential nutrients that are hard to find in plant-based foods.

Pork

Classed as a red meat, pork is high in many vitamins and minerals, including thiamine, zinc, vitamin B12, vitamin B6, niacin, phosphorus and iron. Often cured in the Mediterranean, traditionally pork curing would have been a relatively healthy way to preserve meat. Now, with the advent of preservatives, it is important, if you can, to source cured meats without any chemical additives.

FISH

Fish is a delicious source of protein and essential fatty acids, which support brain and joint health. Although mercury content is now a concern, it tends to be more of an issue with larger fish, such as tuna, so limit your intake of these to once or twice a week. Eaten widely in the Mediterranean, fish is a regular part of the diet.

Oily Fish

Oily fish are a rich source of omega-3 fatty acids, vitamin D and selenium, said to guard against cardiovascular disease and dementia. Salmon, mackerel, anchovies and sardines are common oily fish that are good for health. Tuna is only considered an oily fish when cooked fresh, rather than canned. Steam, bake or fry these fish for a light lunch or satisfying dinner.

White Fish

White fish is a versatile and tasty addition to a balanced diet. Cod, haddock, halibut and sole are among the white fish that are healthy sources of low-fat protein as well as B vitamins and phosphorus.

As part of a balanced diet, white fish can be helpful in fighting inflammation and boosting the immune system. As with oily fish, they can be steamed, baked or fried.

SEAFOOD

Mussels, squid and prawns (shrimp) are among the more common seafoods that are widely available to us. Many other Mediterranean delicacies include less well-known seafoods, including sea urchin and sea cucumber, as well as a wide variety of shellfish that come in many shapes and sizes.

Molluscs

There are thousands of species of molluscs, but the ones that we are most likely to eat from the Mediterranean include oysters, squid, scallops, clams and octopus. Molluscs are good sources of iodine, selenium, zinc and potassium, essential minerals for health.

Although many molluscs, such as oysters, can be eaten raw, in the Mediterranean it is more common to find them pan-fried or barbequed.

Crustaceans

Crustaceans include crabs, lobsters, crayfish and prawns (shrimp). They are high
in omega fatty acids and many of the essential amino acids that promote cellular
regeneration and overall health. The best-quality crustaceans will come fresh from
your local fishmonger. Alternatively, you can find more common crustaceans such as
prawns, little shrimps and crab precooked in well-stocked supermarkets. If buying
fresh, rinse and pat dry before cooking. As with all fish and seafood, take care not to
cook crustaceans for too long to avoid their texture becoming rubbery.

DAIRY

The main dairy ingredients that you will find in the Mediterranean are cheese and
yogurt. Young, fresh cheeses such as mozzarella, ricotta and labneh (from soft,
strained yogurt) are tasty additions to many meals, while feta and halloumi are
made from goats' and sheep's milk, making them healthier and easier to digest.
Live fermented yogurt is also packed full of goodness and a welcome addition to
breakfasts, main meals and desserts. Much of the commercial yogurt available does
not contain the healthy, live cultures that make traditional yogurt so good for you. When
shopping, be sure to pick yogurt brands that say 'live' on them.

EGGS

Eggs are eaten throughout the Mediterranean. A healthy source of easy-to-digest
protein, they are versatile and simple to cook. Eggs are used in breakfast recipes such
as shakshuka, as an addition to salads, in main dishes such as frittata and in many
classic cakes and desserts.

GRAINS

Wholegrains figure widely in the Mediterranean diet. Traditional grains included in Mediterranean meals are barley, buckwheat, bulgur wheat, farro, millet, oats and wheat. They are eaten in their whole form in salads and soups or ground into flours to make artisanal bread, pasta, crepes and pastry.

Wholegrains contain many essential nutrients and, when used in moderation as part of a healthy, balanced diet, are a delicious way to sustain energy. When including grain-based products in your diet, it is important to use the best-quality ingredients possible, as inferior quality grain products can be a hindrance to good health.

NUTS AND SEEDS

Nuts and seeds are a great source of protein and essential healthy fats. Mediterraneans use their rich flavour and satisfying texture in dips, desserts and cakes. Often toasted, they can be scattered over dishes or blended with other ingredients to make classic recipes such as pesto and hummus.

BEANS, PULSES AND LEGUMES

Beans, pulses and legumes are common ingredients in the Mediterranean diet. Their inclusion in soups, casseroles, dips and salads add an enjoyable texture and flavour. Pulses are particularly high in folate, iron, calcium, magnesium, zinc and potassium as well as being low in calories and high in complex carbohydrates and fibre, which makes them filling and satisfying.

Beans, pulses and legumes used in Mediterranean cooking include lentils, chickpeas (garbanzos), butter (lima) beans, haricot (navy) beans, black beans, cannellini beans and split peas. You can buy pulses precooked or dried (in which case you will need to soak them overnight before cooking).

CUPBOARD INGREDIENTS

A simple range of cupboard ingredients is a welcome addition to any cook's kitchen. Although Mediterranean cooking consists mostly of fresh ingredients, some olive oil and a few good-quality herbs, spices and sweeteners are also essential.

Olive oil is used throughout the Mediterranean and is well known for being one of the healthiest oils available. You will find olive oil used in Mediterranean cake recipes, as well as savoury dishes and dressings. The healthiest olive oil is labelled 'extra virgin', meaning it is cold-pressed and retains its nutrients.

Dried herbs and spices that are used in Mediterranean cooking include thyme, rosemary, oregano, marjoram, sage, paprika and saffron. Keep them in airtight containers to retain freshness and flavour.

The Mediterranean diet is naturally low in refined sugar. Many dessert recipes rely solely on the natural sweetness of sun-ripened fruit, while others use honey or small quantities of sugar.

LIVING THE MEDITERRANEAN DIET

MEAL PLANNING

Why meal plan? When changing your diet or incorporating new elements into your diet, advance meal planning greatly improves your chances of these changes happening easily and sustainably. Your ability to eat healthily is greatly influenced by the food that is available to you; making sure that you have the ingredients you need will help you feel and look well.

Meal planning for the Mediterranean diet is easy and fun when broken down into three steps:

- Step 1: Recipe Selection
- Step 2: Ingredients Shopping
- Step 3: Meal Preparation

It is important to find the style of meal planning that works best for you. Some people like to plan a month's meals in advance. Others like to plan for a few days at a time. I personally like to meal plan at the beginning of the weekend for the coming week. This gives you time to enjoy choosing recipes, write an ingredients list and shop, ready for the week ahead.

Having the right ingredients in the fridge and pantry is key to your success in incorporating Mediterranean meals into your diet. Whether you are planning meals for a month or just a few days, making sure you have shopped for all the ingredients is vital.

Recipe Selection

Preparing meals is not just about fulfilling the need to fuel ourselves; it is also an enjoyable challenge and expression of creativity. If you are not yet an experienced cook, choose recipes that feel like they would be fun to make. Stretching yourself too far beyond your natural skill level in the beginning will hinder your confidence in the long run. Choose recipes that feel achievable and will bring you an easy sense of satisfaction.

Each week have fun looking for new recipes. Keeping inspired is paramount to sustaining a healthy diet. Browse your recipe books, favourite blogs and websites for delicious and interesting dishes that you feel drawn to. Use sticky notes to mark your recipe-book choices and save any recipes that you find on the internet in a folder. Better still, print out any internet finds so that they are easy to look at when you are choosing and making the recipes.

There are many fun ways to help you choose which recipes to add to your meal plans:

- Keeping a meal diary enables you to look back and remember the meals that you have made and enjoyed in the past and can make again.

- If you cook for others, ask those you live with and visitors who dine with you what they like to eat.

- Keep a list of favourite staple recipes on your fridge, and refer to it regularly for inspiration.

- Use regular theme nights to give you some direction for your recipe searches. For example, Monday – pasta night; Tuesday – fish; Wednesday – chicken; Thursday – vegetarian; Friday – soup; Saturday – seafood; Sunday – casserole.

Cooking with seasonal ingredients makes the most of natural health-boosting nutrients. Look for recipes that use produce available in the shops at that particular time of year, whether it be heirloom tomatoes and peaches in summer, or root vegetables in winter.

Choose recipes that suit your lifestyle. If you are busy during the week, choose quick and easy recipes Monday to Friday, then enjoy yourself at the weekend with recipes that require more steps, longer cooking or are a little more demanding.

Remember that cooking should be fun and creative, with a manageable amount of challenge in line with your skill level. Choose your recipes to suit your personality and lifestyle. Once you have chosen your breakfasts, lunches and dinners, it is time to make your shopping list.

Shopping

Choosing a regular shopping day will help your fridge and pantry stay well stocked. Running out of healthy ingredients can lead to making unhealthy choices, so be prepared.

To make your shopping list, look through each recipe that you have chosen for your meal plan and write down the ingredients. I write down each ingredient with a quantity next to it and if it comes up again in another recipe, I put that quantity next to it too. At the end, I add up all the amounts to make my final shopping list for that week's recipes.

Keep your cupboards well stocked with basic Mediterranean essentials, such as olive oil, dried herbs and spices, anchovies, olives, capers, canned tomatoes and pulses, pasta, sea salt and black pepper corns for grinding. You will be using these ingredients most days and, if you do get caught without some fresh ingredients, you will still have enough to cook with from your cupboard.

Meal Preparation

Preparing your Mediterranean dishes should bring you great pleasure. Not only will the food that you cook taste wonderful, hopefully your health will improve and enjoyment of eating will increase too.

The first step in preparing a meal is to read through the recipes you are following from beginning to end. Pay attention to how long the cooking times are so that you can estimate, along with chopping and other preparation times, how long the meal will take to get to the table. Some recipes will only take 30 minutes to make, while others may take an hour or two – or sometimes even days with advance preparation. Know what you are in for before you start!

With your recipes for the meal to hand, wash and weigh out the ingredients. Doing this ahead of cooking can help to speed up overall preparation time. It also gives you the opportunity to check that you have everything needed for your recipes.

To help things run smoothly, have to hand all the pans, serving dishes and utensils you will need before you start. Rummaging for the right dish at a crucial point during cooking can cause undue stress and may lead to overcooking tender ingredients.

Once you have everything set up, you are ready to enjoy making your meal with ease.

TIPS FOR COOKING

Mediterranean cooking is usually a fairly simple affair. Preparing raw ingredients, as with the many salads, baking, grilling and frying are the most common ways of cooking in the Mediterranean.

As healthy eating requires you to prepare much of your own food, learning to enjoy cooking is essential to long-term health. Many people feel intimidated by the idea of cooking new dishes. You are not alone! However, the satisfaction derived from preparing a new dish successfully is wonderful and worth the effort, both for the taste and the sense of achievement.

One of the great pleasures of cooking is learning the nuances of food preparation. As you grow accustomed to following recipes, you will be able to sense when ingredients look and smell cooked properly. When I first learned to cook, I followed recipes closely for six months. After that I was able to be more spontaneous and relaxed in the kitchen because I had a better natural feel for cooking, simply from experience. If you are new to cooking, you can look forward to this too. If you are already a pro, you will relate to the pleasure that experience brings. As with all skills, cooking requires practice and patience.

Preparing food that can be frozen during the weekend is a great way to save time during the week. Weekends also give you a fun opportunity to make more elaborate breakfasts and desserts for yourself, friends and family.

If you don't mind eating the same dish more than once, plan to make more than you need for one meal. Leftovers are a super-quick and easy meal choice and can often be modified simply by serving different side dishes.

TIPS FOR SHOPPING

Shopping for Mediterranean ingredients should be easy and inspiring. Although the vast majority of the foods you will need in order to enjoy a Mediterranean diet are available in supermarkets and local stores, searching out interesting websites and quirky delicatessens for the more specialist ingredients is also fun.

I find shopping easiest when I divide my shopping list into sections: fresh produce; ingredients to be kept in the fridge; meat and fish; specialist items etc. This is particularly useful if you are shopping in multiple places for your ingredients.

To reap the full rewards of eating in a healthful way, it is important to focus on good-quality ingredients. Buy organic where you can. Smell fresh fruits and vegetables before you buy them – the more aromatic they smell, the more flavourful they will be. Fruits and vegetables are better for us when they are ripe rather than unripe. Keep unripe items out of the fridge to ripen, so that their nutrients are fully activated by the time you come to use them.

TIPS FOR EATING OUT

Eating out is usually easy on the Mediterranean diet. There are many restaurants that specialize in Mediterranean food to choose from. If you are following the Mediterranean diet closely, bear in mind that not all restaurants serving Mediterranean dishes will adhere strictly to the required ingredients.

You may choose to eat a lot of foods from the Mediterranean without being too strict; in which case eating out and vacations are a time to enjoy foods that are not part of your daily diet. Have fun while you are out and return to your healthy eating when you get back home.

BREAKFAST

SHAKSHUKA

Shakshuka is a traditional North African dish. Much healthier than a traditional Western cooked breakfast, this is a delicious dish to savour over the weekend.

Serves 2-3

1 tablespoon extra virgin olive oil

1 small red onion, peeled and diced,
   plus a few onion rings to garnish

½ red pepper, diced

1 garlic clove, peeled, crushed or minced
   (finely chopped)

400 g/14 oz/2⅓ cups canned
   chopped tomatoes

1 tablespoon tomato paste

pinch sea salt

¼ tsp ground cumin

¼ tsp smoked paprika

¼ tsp cayenne pepper (optional)

1 tbsp chopped flat-leaf parsley,
   plus extra for garnish

freshly ground black pepper and
   sea salt, to taste

3 eggs

pita or crusty bread, for serving

Preheat the oven to 190°C/375°F/Gas Mark 5.

Over a medium heat, warm the olive oil in an oven-proof, non-stick frying pan. Add the chopped red onion and pepper, reduce the heat and sauté for 10 minutes until softened. Stir through the garlic and cook for 2 more minutes. Pour in the chopped tomatoes, tomato paste, salt, cumin, smoked paprika and cayenne pepper plus 1 tablespoon of parsley. Bring to the boil, reduce to a simmer and cook for a further 10 minutes.

Remove the pan from the heat. Add pepper and salt to taste. With the back of a spoon, create three shallow indentations in the top of the tomato sauce, and crack the eggs into them. Place the pan in the oven and cook for 8–10 minutes, until the eggs are cooked to your liking. Garnish with parsley leaves and onion rings and serve with pita or crusty bread.

ROASTED TOMATO & MOZZARELLA
Breakfast Bruschetta

Vine tomatoes and mozzarella cheese are synonymous with Italy and the Mediterranean. Many of us are used to sweet breakfasts, but a savoury start to the day is often healthier.

Serves 1

7 cherry tomatoes on the vine
extra virgin olive oil, to drizzle
pinch sea salt
1 slice fresh crusty bread
2–3 slices mozzarella cheese
1 small handful lambs' lettuce (corn salad)
freshly ground black pepper

Preheat the oven to 200°C/400°F/Gas Mark 6.

Place the cherry tomatoes in an ovenproof dish. Drizzle with olive oil and sprinkle over the salt. Cook in the oven for 8–10 minutes until beginning to brown.

Put the slice of bread onto your serving plate. Drizzle with a little more olive oil, add the mozzarella slices and lambs' lettuce (corn salad). Top with the roasted cherry tomatoes and freshly ground black pepper. Serve while the tomatoes are still warm.

MEDITERRANEAN SCRAMBLED EGGS

This satisfying breakfast also makes for a quick and light lunch or supper. All over the world eggs are scrambled in different ways. The saltiness of the feta works beautifully with the sweetness of the red pepper.

Serves 2

2 tsp extra virgin olive oil

¼ red pepper, diced

1 garlic clove, peeled, crushed or minced (finely chopped)

4 eggs, whisked

1 tbsp coriander (cilantro) leaves, chopped, plus extra leaves to garnish

pinch salt

50 g/2 oz feta cheese, finely sliced

toast, to serve

In a frying pan, heat the olive oil over a medium heat. Add the red pepper and cook for 5 minutes until softening. Stir in the garlic and cook for a further 1 minute. Turn the heat down to low and add the whisked eggs, chopped coriander (cilantro) leaves and salt. Stir continually until the eggs are almost cooked. Remove from the heat and stir through the feta cheese, breaking it up as you go.

Serve with toast and, if you like, a fresh tomato salad.

HALLOUMI & SMASHED AVOCADO SANDWICH

If you've never tried fried halloumi, then you are in for a treat with this breakfast. With a taste a little like bacon, the cheese complements the creaminess of the avocado.

Makes 2 sandwiches

1 ripe avocado
pinch salt
1 tsp lemon juice
4 slices halloumi cheese
extra virgin olive oil for drizzling
4 slices spelt or rye bread
4 lettuce leaves
6 slices cucumber
freshly ground black pepper

Using a dessert spoon, scoop the flesh of the avocado from its skin. Put the avocado flesh in a bowl, add the salt and lemon juice and mash with a fork.

Heat a non-stick frying pan over a medium heat. Add the halloumi slices and dry fry for 2–4 minutes until browned, flipping the cheese over halfway through.

Make the sandwiches with a drizzle of olive oil over the bread, followed by the lettuce, smashed avocado, cucumber and fried halloumi. Grind over some black pepper and serve.

GREEK YOGURT
with Honey-poached Nectarine

Poached fruit for breakfast is a delicious start to the day. You can poach a batch of nectarines, as well as other fruit, and keep them in the fridge for up to 5 days.

Serves 2

2 nectarines, peeled

2 tbsp honey plus 2 tsp honey

1 cinnamon stick

300 ml/½ pint/1¼ cups water

20 g/¾ oz/4 tbsp rolled oats

1 tsp extra virgin olive oil

40 g/1½ oz hazelnuts

500 g/1 lb 1 oz/2 cups Greek yogurt

Preheat the oven to 180°C/350°F/Gas Mark 4.

Cut the nectarines in half, removing the stone. Cut each half into 5 wedges. Add to a pan with 2 tablespoons of honey, the cinnamon stick and the water. Bring to the boil, reduce to a simmer and cook with the lid on for 15–20 minutes until tender. Remove from the heat and allow to cool slightly.

In a bowl, mix the oats with the olive oil and remaining 2 teaspoons of honey. Place the hazelnuts in one half of a baking dish and the oat mix in the other half of the baking dish. Cook in the oven for 10–12 minutes until golden. Let the hazelnuts cool slightly and place in a clean dishcloth. To remove the skins, roll the hazelnuts in the dishcloth between your hands. Cut the nuts into halves.

Divide the Greek yogurt between two bowls, top with the nectarine slices along with a little of the poaching juice. Sprinkle over the toasted hazelnuts and oats and serve.

SMOKED SALMON AVOCADO TOASTS

Smoked salmon and avocado is a classic combination loved by many. This breakfast is light but filling. It will keep you going all the way until lunchtime, with no desire to snack.

Makes 3

1 ripe avocado

pinch salt

juice of ½ lime

extra virgin olive oil, to drizzle

3 slices crusty white bread, toasted

150 g/5 oz smoked salmon

cress, to garnish (optional)

Using a tablespoon, scoop the flesh of the avocado from its skin. Put the avocado flesh in a bowl, add the salt and lime juice and mash with a fork.

Drizzle olive oil over the toast. Divide the mashed avocado between the three toast slices and top with smoked salmon and a sprinkling of cress leaves.

LABNEH WITH PEAS & ARUGULA

Labneh originates from the Middle Eastern Mediterranean. Homemade labneh is easy and satisfying to make and will keep in the refrigerator for up to 3 days.

Serves 2-4

For the labneh

500g/18 oz/2 cups Greek yogurt
1 tsp salt

For the topping

75 g/3 oz/½ cup frozen peas, defrosted
extra virgin olive oil, to drizzle
rocket (arugula), to garnish
freshly ground black pepper
toast, to serve

Line a sieve with a double layer of cheesecloth. Leave the cloth hanging over the sides of the sieve. Place the sieve on top of a jug or deep bowl.

Thoroughly stir the salt into the yogurt. Pour the yogurt into the cheesecloth. Bring the corners of the cloth together and twist from the top, gently squeezing to release any excess liquid from the yogurt.

Place the cheesecloth-wrapped yogurt back in the sieve over the bowl and place in the fridge. Allow to drain overnight, or for 8–24 hours, until it reaches the desired consistency. You have made labneh!

Spoon the labneh into a serving bowl. Sprinkle over the peas and drizzle with olive oil. Finish with a garnish of rocket (arugula) leaves and freshly ground black pepper and serve with toast or pita breads.

FIGGY YOGURT POTS

Dried figs and fresh figs taste quite different and both are incredibly good for you. These easy breakfast pots combine the caramel and fresh flavours of the two together.

Makes 3

3 fresh figs
3 dried figs
65 g/2½ oz/½ cup shelled walnuts
500 g/18 oz/2 cups yogurt
chia seeds, to garnish (optional)

Cut the fresh figs into halves, and then cut each half into 6 slices.

Remove the stems of the dried figs and roughly chop.

Place the walnuts on a chopping board and gently break them up with the back of a wooden spoon.

Take 3 glasses and place 4 slices of fresh fig in the bottom of each glass. Next, add a layer of yogurt. Sprinkle over the dried figs and walnuts in each glass, leaving a few walnuts to garnish the top layer. Add another layer of yogurt and top with the remaining slices of fresh fig, walnuts and a sprinkling of chia seeds, if you have them.

SIDES, SAUCES & DIPS

BABA GANOUSH
(Aubergine & Yogurt Dip)

This classic Greek dip is wonderful as a starter or as part of a mezze selection. I also love it as a filling for jacket (baked) potatoes, served alongside a Greek salad.

Makes 1 medium bowl of dip

For the baba ganoush

- 3 large aubergines (eggplants) (approximately 1.5 kg/3 lb 6 oz in total)
- 2 garlic cloves, peeled and crushed or minced (finely chopped)
- 4 tbsp tahini
- 1 tbsp lemon juice
- 1 tsp sea salt
- 2 tbsp plain full-fat yogurt

To garnish

- extra virgin olive oil, to drizzle
- pinch zaatar spice
- fresh basil leaves

- toasted pita breads, to serve

Preheat the oven to 180°C/350°F/Gas Mark 4.

With a sharp knife pierce the aubergines (eggplants) all over, right through to their centres, to help them cook through. Place in the oven and cook for 50–60 minutes until they are beginning to collapse. Remove them from the oven and put them in a bowl, covered in foil, to cool for 20 minutes.

Once the aubergines are cool enough to handle, remove the skin and discard. Roughly chop the aubergine flesh. Add to a food processor along with the garlic, tahini, lemon juice, salt and yogurt. Pulse until nearly smooth.

Serve in a bowl, garnished with a drizzle of olive oil, a sprinkle of zaatar and basil leaves. Enjoy with toasted pita breads.

HUMMUS

You can buy hummus everywhere these days, but there is nothing like making your own. It is so simple and quick that once you have tried it once you won't look back.

Makes 1 medium bowl of dip

For the hummus

1 x 400 g/14 oz canned chickpeas (garbanzos)

1 tbsp tahini

1 small garlic clove, peeled and crushed

juice of 1 lemon

extra virgin olive oil

½ tsp sea salt

To garnish

1 small handful chickpeas (garbanzos)

1 pinch chili powder

rosemary (optional)

Reserve a small handful of chickpeas (garbanzos) for the garnish. Put the remaining chickpeas into a blender with the rest of the hummus ingredients and blend until almost smooth.

Decant the hummus into a serving bowl. Garnish with the remaining chickpeas, a light sprinkle of chili powder and rosemary, if you have it.

TARAMASALATA

You can use smoked or unsmoked cod roe paste in this recipe, which you can find online or from good fishmongers. I have included beetroot juice as an alternative colourant to the artificial ones used in store-bought taramasalata.

Makes 1 medium bowl of dip

70 g/2½ oz/1 cup fresh white breadcrumbs

70 ml/2½ fl oz/⅓ cup lemon juice

250 ml/8 fl oz/1 cup water

125 g/4 oz smoked or unsmoked cod roe paste

¼ tsp beetroot juice (optional)

600 ml/1 pint/2½ cups olive oil

1 black olive and a little chopped fresh parsley, to garnish (optional)

Add the breadcrumbs to a bowl with water and lemon juice and leave to soak for 15 minutes or more.

Blend the bread mixture with the cod roe and beetroot juice if using, until relatively smooth.

With the blender on a medium speed, slowly start pouring in the olive oil. If you put in too much oil at once the mixture will split, so go gently.

Decant the taramasalata into a serving bowl and garnish with an olive and a sprinkle of parsley.

CLASSIC ITALIAN TOMATO SAUCE

This classic tomato sauce is incredibly versatile. You can serve it tossed with pasta or as a sauce for meat and fish dishes. The better quality the tomatoes, the better the flavour.

Serves 6

3 tbsp extra virgin olive oil

1 small onion, finely chopped

2 garlic cloves, peeled and crushed

800 g/28 oz/3⅓ cups canned chopped tomatoes

1 tsp sugar, or other natural sweetener

½ tsp sea salt

juice of ¼ lemon

3 stems fresh basil, finely minced (chopped)

Heat the olive oil in a saucepan over a medium heat. Add the onion, reduce the heat and fry for 5–10 minutes until translucent.

Add the crushed garlic and cook for another minute. Add the tomatoes, sugar or other sweetener, salt, lemon juice and basil stems. Bring to the boil, turn down to a simmer and cook without a lid for 30–40 minutes until the sauce has thickened.

Serve straightaway with pasta, fish or meat, or store in the fridge for up to one week.

ROMESCO SAUCE

Many romesco sauce recipes start with a base of red peppers, but this more traditional recipe uses vine tomatoes. It makes a wonderful dip and can be kept in the refrigerator for up to 7 days.

Makes 1 medium bowl of dipping sauce

2 tbsp plus 120 ml/4 fl oz/½ cup
  extra virgin olive oil

3 vine tomatoes

¼ red pepper

40 g/1½ oz/¼ cup hazelnuts

40 g/1½ oz/¼ cup almonds

1 medium-thick slice of stale crusty white
  bread

2 tbsp red wine vinegar

1 garlic clove, peeled and crushed

¾ tsp sea salt

red chili slices and parsley to garnish, optional

Preheat the oven to 180°C/350°F/Gas Mark 4. Cut a cross in the bottom of each tomato and place them cut-side up along with the red pepper on a baking pan. Drizzle over two tablespoons of olive oil. Roast the tomatoes and pepper for 50-60 minutes until the skin is beginning to blacken a little.

Toast the hazelnuts and almonds in the oven for 8–10 minutes until just browned. Remove and place them on a clean dish towel. Allow to cool slightly and then roll the nuts inside the towel to remove their skins.

Toast the bread. When the tomatoes and pepper are cooked, remove from the oven and allow to cool. Soak the toast in the vinegar.

Once cooled, peel the skin off the tomatoes and pepper. Place in a food processor with the crushed garlic and salt. Blend at a medium speed, slowly drizzling in the olive oil. Add the soaked toast and nuts and blend until the sauce is the desired texture. Garnish with red chili slices and parsley and serve with crusty bread and grilled vegetables.

CHERRY TOMATO & MOZZARELLA SALAD

This beautiful salad makes an exciting addition to any meal. You can eat it simply with toast or as a side with any Italian-inspired meal. You can use red or mixed cherry tomatoes.

Serves 4

For the dressing

1 handful fresh basil leaves, finely chopped

3 tbsp extra virgin olive oil

pinch sea salt

500 g/1 lb 2 oz mozzarella cheese

2 vine tomatoes, sliced

6 cherry tomatoes, halved

balsamic vinegar, for drizzling

With a pestle and mortar, lightly grind the basil leaves, olive oil and salt.

Cut half of the mozzarella into slices. Tear the remaining mozzarella into chunks.

Arrange the vine tomatoes and sliced mozzarella on a serving plate. Scatter the halved cherry tomatoes on top, and finish with the torn mozzarella.

Pour the dressing over the salad and finish with a light drizzle of balsamic vinegar.

COURGETTE (ZUCCHINI) ANTIPASTI

I love the flavour and look of vegetables cooked on a griddle pan. Deceptively simple, this dish makes a colourful addition to an antipasti or mezze selection.

Makes 2-3 servings

1 large courgette (zucchini)

3 tbsp extra virgin olive oil

1 tbsp fresh rosemary leaves

¼ tsp mild chili flakes

pinch sea salt

7 garlic cloves, skins on

zest of ⅓ lemon and fresh thyme sprigs, to garnish

Cut the courgette (zucchini) lengthways into 5 mm/⅕ inch slices.

Combine the olive oil, rosemary, chili and salt in a mixing bowl. Toss the courgette slices and garlic cloves in the marinade and leave to stand for 10 minutes.

Heat a griddle pan over a medium heat. Place the slices of courgette in the pan and cook for about 5 minutes on each side until charred stripes appear.

Serve sprinkled with lemon zest and sprigs of fresh thyme.

GRIDDLED AUBERGINE (EGGPLANT)
with Yogurt

This dish can be served as a side dish or as a light main meal, alongside hummus and pita breads. Pomegranates are incredibly good for you, as well as looking pretty here.

Makes 2–4 servings

1 medium aubergine (eggplant)

2 tbsp extra virgin olive oil

1 tsp lemon juice

¼ tsp sea salt

To garnish

4 tbsp yogurt

½ tsp dried oregano

5 tbsp pomegranate seeds

a few fresh coriander (cilantro) leaves

a few fresh parsley leaves,
    finely chopped

a few walnuts, finely chopped

Slice the aubergine (eggplant) lengthways into 4 slices of equal thickness.

Combine the olive oil, lemon juice and salt together and brush over both sides of the aubergine slices.

Heat a griddle pan over a medium-high heat. Place the aubergine slices in the pan and cook for 5 minutes on each side until char lines appear and the aubergine is just cooked.

Serve hot, topped with a spoonful of yogurt, a little dried oregano, a generous sprinkling of pomegranate seeds, fresh coriander (cilantro) and parsley and a few chopped walnuts.

SOUPS & LIGHT MEALS

BOUILLABAISSE

Originating from the Provençal port city of Marseille, this fish stew is delicately flavoured with herbs, spices and vegetables.

Serves 4

For the broth

500 ml/18 fl oz/2 cups homemade or
   store-bought fish stock

2 tbsp tomato paste

2 pinches saffron

2 tarragon sprigs, leaves only

juice of 2 lemons

1 tbsp pastis or Pernod (optional)

40 g/1½ oz/3 tbsp butter

sea salt and freshly ground black pepper

For the rouille

3 egg yolks

¼ tsp sea salt

pinch freshly ground black pepper

1 lemon, juiced

pinch saffron

pinch cayenne pepper

200 ml/7 fl oz/¾ cup extra virgin olive oil

200 ml/7 fl oz/¾ cup light vegetable oil

4 garlic cloves, peeled and crushed

To serve

2 tbsp extra virgin olive oil, plus more for drizzling

1 onion, peeled and finely diced

½ fennel bulb, cored and finely diced

2 garlic cloves, peeled and crushed or finely minced (chopped)

1 fresh plum tomato, peeled, deseeded and finely chopped

300 g/11 oz pollock, skinned

300 g/11 oz monkfish, skinned

8 shell-on fresh king prawns (jumbo shrimp), rinsed

8 mussels, cleaned

1 small sprig parsley leaves, finely chopped, to garnish

Blend the broth ingredients to a smooth sauce, adding salt and pepper to taste.

To make the rouille, slowly blend the egg yolks with the seasoning, lemon
juice, saffron and cayenne pepper. Slowly add the oil in a thin stream, blending
continuously. Add the garlic and add a little warm water to thin it down if you need to.
Set aside until required.

Cut the fish into generous bite-size pieces and season lightly with salt and pepper.

Heat the olive oil in a large saucepan over a medium heat. Add the onion and fennel,
turn down the heat and cook for 10 minutes, stirring regularly. Add the garlic and cook
for a further 2 minutes. Pour in the bouillabaisse broth and bring to a simmer. Add 2
tablespoons of the rouille and whisk well. Stir in the finely chopped tomato.

Add the fish, prawns and mussels to the broth and poach gently for 10 minutes until
just cooked, removing any unopened mussels. Serve immediately topped with a little
chopped parsley, crusty fresh bread and remaining rouille.

ITALIAN MINESTRONE SOUP

Minestrone soup is a well-loved classic for a reason. Here I have used elbow pasta, but you can get creative with the kind you use. Bow and shell pastas also work well.

Serves 6

4 tbsp extra virgin olive oil

1 medium onion, peeled and chopped

2 medium carrots, chopped

2 medium celery ribs, chopped

1 red pepper, deseeded and chopped

1 yellow pepper, deseeded and chopped

4 cloves garlic, peeled and crushed or minced (finely chopped)

1 tsp dried oregano

2 bay leaves

mild chili flakes

800g/28 oz /3⅓ cups canned chopped tomatoes

1 litre/1¾ pints/4 cups vegetable stock

500 ml/18 fl oz/2 cups water

1 tsp sea salt

4 tbsp tomato paste

freshly ground black pepper

150 g/5 oz/1⅓ cup elbow or small shell pasta

75 g/3 oz/½ cup fresh green beans, chopped

150 g/5 oz/1 cup frozen peas

400 g/14 oz/2½ cups canned cannellini beans, drained

2 tsp lemon juice

Heat the olive oil in a soup pan over a medium heat. Add the chopped onion, carrots, celery and red and yellow peppers and cook for 10 minutes, stirring regularly.

Add the garlic, oregano, bay leaves and chili flakes. Cook for a further 2 minutes.

Pour in the canned tomatoes, stock and water. Stir in the salt and tomato paste. Season generously with freshly ground black pepper and bring to the boil. Reduce to a gentle simmer and cook for 15 minutes with the lid slightly ajar.

Add the pasta, green beans, peas and cannellini beans. Continue simmering, uncovered, for 20 minutes until the pasta is cooked *al dente*.

Remove from the heat. Take out the bay leaves and stir in the lemon juice. Season with salt and pepper to taste. Serve immediately with crusty bread.

ROASTED RED PEPPER, TOMATO & RED ONION SOUP

Full of flavour and a rich, tempting colour, this Mediterranean soup is packed full of goodness. Serve it as a starter or for a light lunch.

Serves 4

2 large red peppers, deseeded and roughly chopped

1 red onion, peeled and roughly chopped

2 tbsp extra virgin olive oil

3 tomatoes, halved

1 tsp sea salt, plus extra for seasoning

1 garlic clove, peeled and crushed

600 ml/1 pint/2½ cups vegetable stock

1 tsp Worcestershire sauce

freshly ground black pepper

4 tbsp single (light) cream or oat cream

rosemary sprigs, to garnish

Preheat the oven to 190C°/375°F/Gas Mark 5.

Toss the red peppers and red onion in the olive oil and place in a single layer on a baking tray. Cook in the oven for 10 minutes. Add the tomatoes and cook for a further 20 minutes until the peppers are soft.

Once cooked, remove the vegetables from the oven and allow to cool slightly. Add the cool vegetables to a blender with 1 teaspoon of the salt, the garlic, vegetable stock and Worcestershire sauce. Season with pepper and extra salt to taste.

Heat the soup gently until piping hot. Pour into bowls. Drizzle a spoonful of cream into each bowl and garnish with rosemary before serving.

QUICK MEDITERRANEAN PRAWNS

Caught in the morning and eaten in the evening, this is the healthy way the
Mediterranean people enjoy their seafood starters and main dishes.

Serves 2

12 large raw prawns (jumbo shrimp)
1 tbsp olive oil
1 garlic clove, peeled and crushed
1 slice lemon, halved
2 basil leaves, shredded
a little fresh red chili, finely chopped, to taste (optional)
pinch sea salt
fresh coriander (cilantro) leaves to garnish

Remove the shells from the prawns (jumbo shrimp), leaving the tail shells on. Using a
small sharp knife, remove the dark vein that runs along the underside of the prawns.
Rinse and drain on absorbent paper towels.

In a small mixing bowl, mix the olive oil with the garlic, lemon, basil leaves, chili
(if using), and salt. Add the prawns and toss to coat them in the marinade.

Place a frying pan over a high heat. Add the prawns and marinade to the pan and fry
for 3–4 minutes, or until the prawns are pink and just cooked through, stirring every
minute or so.

Arrange the prawns on a platter and garnish with a little fresh coriander (cilantro).

SPINACH & GREEN BEAN FRITTATA

Frittatas are a like a pastry-free quiche. This recipe is delicious as it is, and also fun to adapt depending on what ingredients you have in the refrigerator.

Makes 3-4 servings

8 organic eggs

120 ml/4 fl oz/½ cup milk, dairy or dairy free

2 garlic cloves, peeled and crushed or minced (finely chopped)

½ tsp sea salt

freshly ground black pepper

50 g/2 oz feta cheese

2 tbsp extra virgin olive oil

1 small onion, peeled and chopped

6 tbsp water

150 g/6 oz/1 cup fresh green beans, chopped

65 g/2½ oz/2 cups baby spinach, roughly chopped

Preheat the oven to 220°C/425°F/Gas Mark 7.

In a large bowl, thoroughly whisk together the eggs, milk, garlic and salt and season with freshly ground black pepper. Next, whisk in the feta cheese.

In a 25 cm/10 inch oven-safe non-stick frying pan, heat the olive oil over a medium heat. Add the onion and cook, stirring frequently, for 5–7 minutes until tender and translucent.

Add the water and green beans to the pan and cover with a lid. Steam for 3–5 minutes until the beans can be easily pierced with a fork. Add the spinach and cook for another minute, stirring constantly, until the spinach has wilted.

Arrange the vegetables in an even layer in the frying pan. Whisk the egg mixture one last time and pour it into the pan. Put the pan in the oven and bake for 12–15 minutes until the frittata is set in the middle.

Remove the pan from the oven and allow to rest for 5 minutes before serving.

Leftover frittata will keep in the refrigerator for up to 3 days and is great for packed lunches.

SPINACH, FETA & OLIVE PARCELS

These cute parcels are perfect for nibbles at a drinks party. There is no need to add salt as olives and feta are quite salty. Your guests won't resist eating more than one!

Makes 30

4 tbsp extra virgin olive oil

1 small red pepper, diced

1 small yellow pepper, diced

4 fresh thyme sprigs

2 garlic cloves, peeled and crushed

225 g/8 oz/7½ cups baby spinach, roughly chopped

50 g/2 oz/¼ cups assorted green and black olives, pitted

125 g/4½ oz feta cheese

2 tbsp pine nuts, lightly toasted

freshly ground black pepper

6 sheets filo (phyllo) pastry

Preheat the oven to 180°C/350°F/Gas Mark 4.

Add 1 tbsp olive oil to a frying pan. Tip in the red and yellow peppers. Cook, stirring regularly, for 10 minutes. Strip the leaves from the thyme sprigs, adding them to the pan with the garlic. Cook for a further 2 minutes. Stir in the spinach and cook for another minute, stirring gently until the spinach has wilted.

Chop the olives and feta cheese into small cubes. In a mixing bowl, combine the olives, feta, spinach mixture and pine nuts. Season with black pepper.

Cut a sheet of filo (phyllo) pastry in quarters. Brush with olive oil. For the first layer of the parcel, place a heaped teaspoon of the vegetable and feta mixture into the centre of the sheet. Fold the pastry over to enclose the filling completely.

Brush a second piece of filo pastry on both sides with olive oil. Place the first parcel in the centre and bring the corners of the second sheet up to meet in the middle, twisting loosely to close. Gently place the twisted parcel on a lightly oiled baking sheet. Continue until all the parcels are made.

Bake in the preheated oven for 10–15 minutes until crisp and golden brown. Serve warm.

GRIDDLED GARLIC & LEMON SQUID

Searching for squid in the rocks is a pastime undertaken by many a Mediterranean youth; not surprising if they get to eat this tasty dish.

Serves 4

225 g/8 oz squid, cleaned
2 tsp olive oil
finely grated zest of 1 lemon
2 garlic cloves, peeled and crushed
sea salt and freshly ground black pepper
2 tbsp fresh basil, chopped
2 tbsp lemon juice

To prepare the squid, peel the tentacles from the squid's pouch and cut away the header just below the eye. Discard the header. Remove the quill and the soft innards from the squid and discard. Peel off any dark skin that covers the squid and discard. Rinse the tentacles and pouch thoroughly. The squid is now ready to use.

Remove the tentacles from the squid and reserve. Using the tip of a small sharp knife, score the flesh of the body cavity, without cutting all the way through.

Mix the olive oil, lemon zest and crushed garlic with some salt and pepper. Place the squid and its tentacles in a shallow bowl, sprinkle over the lemon mixture and stir.

Heat a griddle pan until almost smoking. Cook the squid for 3–5 minutes until just cooked through. Sprinkle with the basil and lemon juice. Serve hot with salad and griddled tomatoes.

MEDITERRANEAN CHOWDER

With the Mediterranean Sea on their doorsteps, little wonder that this is a popular, healthy and wholesome fish-based soup or stew in many Mediterranean countries.

Serves 6

3 tbsp olive oil

1 large onion, peeled and diced

2 medium carrots, diced

1 medium yellow pepper, diced

225 g/8 oz/1 cup potatoes, diced

1 mild or medium heat yellow chili

2 garlic cloves, peeled and crushed
    or minced (finely chopped)

75 g/3 oz/⅔ cup cauliflower, chopped

1 litre/1¾ pints/4 cups fish stock

350 g/12 oz whiting or cod fillet

350 g/12 oz fresh tuna

sea salt and freshly ground black pepper

2 tbsp fresh parsley, chopped

fresh parsley leaves, to garnish

Heat the oil in a large saucepan, add the onion, carrots, yellow pepper and potatoes and fry gently for 10 minutes, stirring regularly. Cut the chili into narrow rings. Add the garlic and chilli to the pan and cook for a further minute. Add the cauliflower to the saucepan with the stock. Bring to the boil, cover and simmer for 10 minutes until the potatoes are cooked through.

Cut the fish into large bite-size pieces.

Season the chowder to taste with salt and pepper. Stir in the chopped parsley before adding the fish to the saucepan. Bring to the boil, reduce to a simmer and cook with the lid on for a further 5–10 minutes until the fish is just done. Ladle into soup bowls, garnish with fresh parsley leaves and serve immediately.

MAINS: SALADS & VEGETABLES

PRAWN & GRAPEFRUIT SALAD

This simple and fresh salad is a great dish for a light and healthy lunch. If you've never segmented a grapefruit before there are some great how-to videos on the internet.

Serves 2-4

2 little gem (baby gem) lettuces

1 pink grapefruit, peeled and segmented

1 avocado, pitted, peeled and sliced

350 g/12 oz cooked prawns (shrimp)

sea salt

1 tsp black sesame seeds (optional)

extra virgin olive oil, to drizzle

Separate the leaves of the little gem lettuces and arrange on 2–4 plates or one bigger serving platter. Next, add the pink grapefruit segments and avocado slices. Scatter over the cooked prawns (shrimp). Sprinkle over a little sea salt to taste and finish with black sesame seeds, if using. Drizzle over a little olive oil before serving.

Serve simply as it is, or with a squeeze of lemon juice, a drizzle of olive oil and some crusty bread and butter.

NEW POTATO & ANCHOVY SALAD

This filling salad works well as a packed lunch, or as a side dish to meat or fish alongside a green salad or steamed greens. You will find marinated anchovies in good delicatessens.

Serves 2-4

500 g/1 lb 2 oz new potatoes

½ cucumber

1 small bunch chives, snipped

1 tsp dried mixed herbs

10 marinated anchovies

2 tbsp extra virgin olive oil

2 tsp white wine vinegar

sea salt and pepper, to season

Bring a pan of salted water to the boil. Cut the new potatoes into pieces roughly 2.5 cm/1 inch in size and add to the boiling water. Bring back to the boil, reduce to a simmer and cook for 10 minutes until just cooked. Drain the potatoes and refresh with cold water to stop them cooking and to cool them down. Drain once cooled.

Halve and then quarter the cucumber lengthways and cut into slices. Add them to a serving bowl with the potatoes, snipped chives, dried herbs and anchovies.

Combine the olive oil, white wine vinegar, salt and pepper in a small bowl. Pour over the salad and mix gently with a large spoon.

Serve as a light main meal or as a side dish.

CHICKEN FETA SALAD

Packed full of protein, this salad is great if you are trying to lose weight or maintain a healthy weight. The protein content will keep you full and give you energy to sustain you through the day.

Serves 1

For the salad

2.5 cm/1 inch cucumber, halved lengthways and sliced

3 cherry tomatoes, halved

2 red onion rings, finely sliced

2.5 cm/1 inch leek, finely sliced

few rocket (arugula) leaves

¼ tsp dried mint

50 g/2 oz feta cheese, cut into cubes

2 tsp extra virgin olive oil

sea salt and freshly ground black pepper

fresh parsley, to garnish

For the chicken

¼ tsp paprika

1 tbsp extra virgin olive oil

1 tsp lemon juice

¼ tsp sea salt

freshly ground black pepper

1 chicken breast

In a mixing bowl, combine the paprika, olive oil, lemon juice, salt and pepper to make a marinade. Cut the chicken breast into slices and toss in the marinade. Leave to stand for 10 minutes or more.

While the chicken is marinating, combine the salad ingredients in a bowl.

Heat a frying pan over a medium heat. Add the chicken slices and cook for 12–15 minutes, turning from time to time, until cooked through. Add the chicken to the salad, garnish with parsley and serve while the chicken is still warm.

CLASSIC GREEK SALAD

In this recipe, I have used a combination of red and green oakleaf lettuce, but feel free to use your favourite lettuce instead. Good-quality olives are a must here.

Serves 2-4

4 cherry tomatoes, quartered

¼ cucumber, halved and sliced

4 lettuce leaves, torn

¼ red pepper, deseeded, quartered and sliced

¼ red onion, finely sliced

8 good-quality green olives

100 g/3½ oz feta cheese, cubed

1 tbsp extra virgin olive oil

Combine all the ingredients in a bowl. For a light lunch, divide the salad between two dinner plates and serve with bread or pitas. As a side dish, serve in a salad bowl or platter to accompany other Greek-inspired recipes.

SALADE NIÇOISE

This healthy Niçoise salad dish combines many of the ingredients that are cultivated in most Mediterranean countries. This is another great salad for healthy weight loss or maintenance.

Serves 2-4

1 egg

30 g/1¼ oz/2 tbsp canned anchovy fillets

8 ripe cherry tomatoes

¼ red onion, peeled and finely chopped

50 g/2 oz/⅓ cup black pitted olives

200 g/7 oz/1 cup canned tuna in water, drained

1 small green lettuce, washed

extra virgin olive oil for drizzling

1 spring onion (scallion), chopped

freshly ground black pepper

Boil the egg for 10 minutes, then rinse thoroughly under a cold running tap until cool. Remove the shell under water and cut the egg in half lengthways, and then cut each half into thirds.

Put five anchovies to one side. In a mixing bowl, combine the cherry tomatoes, red onion, olives, tuna and remaining anchovies, lightly breaking up the tuna as you go.

Separate the lettuce leaves and arrange in a serving bowl. Pile the tuna and olive mix on top of the lettuce. Drizzle with olive oil. Sprinkle the spring onion (scallion) over and arrange the egg and remaining anchovies on top. Season with freshly ground black pepper and serve with crusty bread, drizzled with extra olive oil.

Provence, olivier, Ulivo,
frantoio. Olive oil.

ROAST VEGETABLE & FETA SALAD

Roast vegetables are so versatile. I often roast a whole batch and keep it in the refrigerator to add to salads and as a side dish with meat and fish. They keep well for up to 4 days.

Serves 2-4

1 medium red onion, peeled and cut into bite-size pieces

1 small aubergine (eggplant), cut into bite-size pieces

1 medium courgette (zucchini), cut into bite-size pieces

2 tbsp extra virgin olive oil

¼ tsp sea salt

freshly ground black pepper

2 tsp balsamic vinegar

12 cherry tomatoes on the vine

2 fresh thyme sprigs

50 g/2 oz/⅓ cup pitted Kalamata olives

100 g/3½ oz feta cheese, cubed

Preheat the oven to 180°C/350°F/Gas Mark 4.

In a roasting pan, mix together the red onion, aubergine (eggplant), courgette (zucchini), olive oil, salt, pepper and balsamic vinegar. Cook in the oven for 30 minutes, stirring the vegetables once after 15 minutes of cooking.

Remove 6 of the cherry tomatoes from the vine and stir into the roasting pan. Coat the remaining cherry tomatoes in a thin layer of olive oil and place on top of the roasted vegetables in the pan with the thyme sprigs. Cook for a further 10 minutes.

Remove from the oven and scatter over the olives and feta cheese. Serve hot or cold as a side dish or light main meal.

FRENCH ONION TART

This is such a special dish. Serve it with a fresh green salad and some quality French mustard. I have used white onions in this recipe, but it works equally well with red onions.

Serves 3-4

500 g/1 lb 2 oz–600 g/1 lb 5 oz small to medium whole onions, peeled
75 g/3 oz/6 tbsp salted butter
2 tsp fresh thyme leaves
200 g/7 oz puff pastry

Preheat the oven to 200°C/400°F/Gas Mark 6.

Halve the peeled onions across their centres. Over a medium heat, melt the butter in a 20 cm/8-inch non-stick, oven-proof frying pan. Place the onions in the pan, cut-side down, filling it snuggly. Turn the heat down and cook for 15–20 minutes until the bottoms of the onions are golden. Gently turn them over, adding the thyme, and continue cooking until the onions are fully cooked and soft. Turn the onions back over. Turn off the heat and allow to cool for 15 minutes.

Roll the pastry out to a 23 cm/9 inch circle. Place it on top of the onions and tuck the edges into the side of the pan. Bake for 20–30 minutes until the pastry is puffed and golden. Remove from the oven and cool slightly.

To plate up, place a large plate over the top of the pan. Quickly and firmly turn the pan and plate over so that the plate is on the bottom. Shake slightly to loosen the tart and remove the pan, loosening any stuck onions with a spatula. Serve warm with a green salad.

MUSHROOM GALETTE

Galettes are traditional French crepes made using buckwheat flour. You can fill them with whatever you fancy, but this mushroom and cheese filling is just divine.

Makes 6

For the galettes

150 g/5 oz/1¼ cup buckwheat flour

1 egg

pinch sea salt

300 ml/½ pint/1¼ cups water

25 g/1 oz/2 tbsp butter

For the filling

25 g/1 oz/2 tbsp butter

2 garlic cloves, peeled and crushed or minced (finely chopped)

275 g/10 oz/4 cups chestnut/cremini mushrooms, sliced

2 tsp dill, roughly chopped

125 g/4½ oz/½ cup soft white cheese

To serve (optional)

chives

cherry tomatoes

baby spinach

For the galettes, combine the buckwheat flour, egg, salt and 150 ml water in a blender until smooth. Place the galette batter in a sealed container in the refrigerator for 24 hours.

Before cooking, blend the batter with the remaining 150 ml of water until smooth.

To make the filling, melt the butter over a medium heat. Add the garlic and cook for 1 minute. Mix in the mushrooms and cook for 5 minutes. Stir through the dill, remove from the heat and keep warm while you cook the galettes.

Add 1 tbsp of butter to a non-stick frying pan over a medium heat. Once melted and just bubbling, pour in about 120 ml/4 fl oz/½ cup of the galette batter. Hold the pan by the handle and move it around to spread the mixture into an even circle.

Place one sixth of the mushroom mix plus one sixth of the cheese into the centre of the galette and let everything cook for 2 minutes. Fold in the sides of the galette to make a square and place on a plate to keep warm in the oven. When ready to serve, garnish with chives, cherry tomatoes and baby spinach or serve with a green salad.

AUBERGINE CANNELLONI

This low-carbohydrate version of the traditional Italian cannelloni makes for an easy-to-digest dinner. It freezes well, so make it at the weekend for eating during the week.

Serves 8

4 aubergines (eggplants), cut into thin slices lengthways

4 tbsp extra virgin olive oil, plus more for frying

1 red onion, peeled and finely diced

2 garlic cloves, peeled and crushed or minced (chopped)

2 tsp dried oregano

800 g/28 oz/3⅓ cups canned chopped tomatoes

200 g/7 oz mushrooms

225 g/8 oz halloumi cheese, cut into 1 cm cubes

500 g/1 lb 2 oz spinach

sea salt and freshly ground pepper to season

3 tbsp melting cheese, grated

fresh oregano leaves, to garnish

Heat the oven to 220°C/425°F/Gas Mark 7.

Brush both sides of the aubergine (eggplant) slices with olive oil. Lay on a large baking sheet and bake for 15–20 mins until tender, turning once.

Heat a generous drizzle of olive oil in a frying pan over a medium heat. Add the onions and sauté for 5–7 minutes until translucent. Add the garlic and oregano and cook for one more minute. Stir in the tomatoes, bring to the boil and simmer for 7–10 minutes until the sauce has thickened.

Meanwhile, fry the mushrooms in olive oil over a medium heat for 4 minutes, stirring regularly. Remove the mushrooms, wipe the pan, then add the halloumi cubes. Fry until lightly golden and put to one side.

Put the spinach in a large colander. Pour over boiling water to wilt. Cool, then squeeze out the excess water. Stir into the tomato mix with the mushrooms and plenty of seasoning.

Dollop a spoonful of the tomato-mushroom-spinach mix into the centre of each aubergine slice. Sprinkle over the halloumi cubes and fold over to make a parcel. Lay sealed-side down in a greased ovenproof dish. Sprinkle with grated cheese and bake for 20–25 mins until golden. Serve piping hot with a sprinkling of oregano leaves on top.

QUICK RATATOUILLE

A classic Provençale dish, this is served hot or cold, as an accompaniment to meat or fish, or as a meal on its own with crusty bread and butter.

Serves 4-6

2 courgettes (zucchini), trimmed

1 small aubergine (eggplant), trimmed

1 tbsp extra virgin olive oil

1 red pepper, deseeded and diced

3 garlic cloves, peeled and minced (finely chopped)

3 basil leaves, freshly chopped

1 tbsp parsley, freshly chopped

salt and freshly ground black pepper

Cut the courgettes (zucchini) and aubergine (eggplant) into bite-size pieces. Heat the olive oil in a frying pan over a medium heat. Add the vegetables and cook for 10 minutes, stirring regularly. Add the garlic, stirring for 30 seconds. Turn down the heat, cover and simmer for 15 minutes, or until the vegetables are tender. Stir in the fresh herbs, leaving a little for garnishing. Season to taste with salt and pepper.

Serve the ratatouille hot or cold as a main dish with rice or crusty bread, or as a side dish with meat or fish.

PASTA PRIMAVERA

This lovely looking pasta dish makes me smile every time I serve it. The different shades of green conjure up the joy of spring, whatever the time of year.

Serves 2

175 g/6 oz/1 cup broccoli florets

200 g/7 oz tagliatelle verdi or plain tagliatelle

3 tbsp extra virgin olive oil

1 garlic clove, peeled and crushed or minced (finely chopped)

1 tsp mixed herbs

450 g/1 lb baby spinach

150 g/5 oz/1 cup frozen (defrosted) or fresh peas

Steam the broccoli florets for 5–7 minutes until just turning bright green. Remove from the heat and refresh under cold water to stop the broccoli from cooking.

Bring a large pan of salted water to the boil and add the tagliatelle. Cook according to the packet instructions.

Heat the olive oil in a large frying pan over a medium heat. Add the garlic and mixed herbs and cook, stirring, for 1 minute. Add the spinach, broccoli and peas and cook, stirring, for 3–5 minutes until the spinach is wilted and the broccoli and peas are heated through. Season with salt and pepper to taste.

Drain the pasta, toss with the vegetables and oil from the pan and serve immediately.

PASTA WITH FRESH TOMATO SAUCE

This dish is all about the quality of the tomatoes, so make it when you discover a gorgeous source of this summer bounty. It is delicious with a generous grating of fresh Parmesan too.

Serves 2

6 medium vine tomatoes

50 g/2 oz/⅓ cup Kalamata olives, pitted

225 g/8 oz spaghetti

2 tbsp extra virgin olive oil

1 garlic clove, peeled and crushed

¼ yellow pepper, deseeded and
    finely diced

1 tbsp capers

1 tsp lemon juice

½ tsp demerara (turbinado)
    sugar or natural sweetener

sea salt and freshly ground
    black pepper

basil leaves, to garnish

Put a large pan of salted water on to boil.

Cut a shallow cross into the bottom of each tomato. Put into a bowl or pan with just-boiled water and leave to stand for 5 minutes. Peel off the skins and dice the tomatoes. Chop the olives.

Put the spaghetti on to cook in the large pan of boiling water.

Heat the olive oil in a frying pan over a medium heat. Add the garlic and cook, stirring, for 1 minute. Add the yellow pepper and cook for a further 5 minutes. Add the tomatoes, olives, capers, lemon juice and sugar and cook for another 5–7 minutes, stirring regularly, until the tomatoes are starting to collapse. Season with salt and pepper to taste.

Drain the pasta. Drizzle over some olive oil and season with salt and pepper to taste. Toss the sauce and pasta together. Serve immediately, topped with fresh basil leaves to garnish.

STUFFED PEPPERS

Stuffed peppers are delicious at any time of year. I have used yellow peppers and goats'
cheese in this recipe, but you can substitute red peppers and feta as an alternative.

Serves 2-4

2 yellow peppers

1 small bunch fresh basil

1 tbsp extra virgin olive oil

1 medium onion, peeled and finely chopped

2 garlic cloves, peeled and crushed or minced (finely chopped)

1 tsp dried oregano

6 cherry tomatoes, sliced

12 pitted black olives

sea salt and freshly ground black pepper

100 g/3½ oz soft goats' cheese

parsley leaves, to garnish (optional)

Preheat the oven to 200°C/400°F/Gas Mark 6.

Cut the yellow peppers in half from top to bottom and discard the seeds. With the open
side up, place them on a baking tray. If necessary, slice a fine slither from the base of
the peppers to help them stay flat. Bake for 15 minutes.

Pick the basil leaves from their stems and put a few leaves aside for garnishing later.

Heat the olive oil over a medium heat and add the onion. Cook, stirring regularly, for
4–5 minutes until softened. Add the garlic and oregano and cook for another minute,
stirring constantly. Remove from the heat and stir in the sliced cherry tomatoes, olives
and basil leaves. Season with salt and pepper to taste.

Break up the goats' cheese into small bite-size pieces and stir gently into the mix.

Fill the peppers with the mixture and return to the oven for 10 minutes, or until the peppers are softened and the filling is lightly browned on top.

Eat hot or cold with a garnish of fresh basil leaves, and parsley if you have it. Stuffed peppers are delicious with toast drizzled with olive oil, or with a selection of salads.

VEGETABLE TAGINE

When I visited Morocco, I enjoyed many takes on the traditional Moroccan tagine. This version is a vegetarian delight and looks good enough for a royal feast.

Serves 4

4 tbsp extra virgin olive oil

1 medium onion, peeled and sliced

3 garlic cloves, peeled and crushed
   or minced (finely chopped)

½ tsp ground turmeric

½ tsp ground cinnamon

½ tsp ground cumin

1 tsp ground coriander

2 tbsp tomato paste

1–2 tsp harissa paste

3 medium carrots

1 medium aubergine (eggplant)

2 medium courgette (zucchini)

75 g/3 oz/½ cup fresh or frozen peas

500 ml/18 fl oz/2 cups vegetable stock

sea salt and freshly ground black pepper

1 tsp fresh parsley, finely minced (chopped)

1 tsp fresh mint, finely minced (chopped)

couscous, to serve

Pour the olive oil into the base of a tagine or heavy based saucepan with a lid. Arrange the onion in the bottom.

Combine the garlic and spices in a mixing bowl, with the tomato paste and 1 or 2 teaspoons of harissa depending how much chili heat you like. Add the vegetables and mix well. Arrange the vegetables in a conical shape on top of the onions.

Add the vegetable stock, salt and pepper. Cover, and place over medium-low heat. Bring slowly to a simmer, about 20 minutes. Once simmering, continue to cook over medium-low heat for 20 minutes until the vegetables are very tender. Check every now and then to make sure the vegetables are not burning, turning down the heat if necessary.

Serve hot, sprinkled with chopped parsley and mint, with couscous.

MAINS: FISH & SEAFOOD

BAKED FISH
with Sun-Dried Tomatoes & Olives

This sumptuous dish can be made with many different types of fish fillet. Depending on how thick your fish fillets are, you may need to adjust the time in the oven. Dunk bread into the sauce!

Serves 3–4

4 tbsp extra virgin olive oil

2 garlic cloves, peeled and crushed

6 sun-dried tomatoes in oil

2 tsp lemon juice

sea salt and freshly ground black pepper

600 g/1 lb 5 oz white fish fillets,
   such as haddock or pollock

8 cherry tomatoes, sliced

8 kalamata olives, pitted

1 tsp mixed herbs

lemon wedges and fresh
   parsley, to garnish

crusty toast, to serve

Preheat the oven to 190°C/375°F/Gas Mark 5.

Mash 3 tablespoons of the olive oil with the garlic, three sun-dried tomatoes and lemon juice into a paste in a pestle and mortar or small food processor. Season with salt and pepper. Place the marinade in a bowl with the fish fillets and leave for 10 minutes.

Pour 1 tablespoon of olive oil evenly into a baking dish. Cover the bottom loosely with the cherry tomatoes and olives, reserving a few to scatter over the fish later. Place the fish and marinade on top of the olives and tomatoes. Sprinkle over the mixed herbs, the reserved cherry tomatoes and olives and bake in the oven for 15–20 minutes until the fish is just cooked.

Remove from the oven, garnish with lemon wedges and fresh parsley and serve immediately with crusty toast and a fresh green salad.

CLASSIC GRILLED FISH

Fishmongers have a wealth of knowledge when it comes to preparing and cooking fish and seafood. Be sure to ask your fishmonger how long it takes to cook your whole fish.

Serves 1-2

1 medium-size whole fish, such as sea bream (porgy) or bass, gutted

a drizzle extra virgin olive oil

small pinch sea salt

2 cherry tomatoes, quartered

2 artichoke hearts, quartered

4 green olives

fresh herb sprigs and a lemon slice, to garnish

Preheat the oven to 200°C/400°F/Gas Mark 6.

Rub a drizzle of olive oil and a pinch of salt over the skin of the fish. Place on a baking tray and cook in the oven for 20 minutes until the flesh flakes easily.

Arrange your cooked fish on a plate with the cherry tomatoes, artichoke hearts and olives, finishing off with a few sprigs of fresh herbs and a slice of lemon. Eat with crusty bread and olive oil or with new potatoes and a green salad.

SEAFOOD SALAD

This spectacular and special seafood salad requires some patience but is well worth the effort. You can buy frozen octopus online, along with other harder-to-find seafood. This salad is delicious with extra squid instead of octopus too.

Serves 4

150 g/5 oz fresh or frozen shelled king prawns (jumbo shrimp)

150 g/5 oz frozen octopus tentacles

1 bay leaf

2 garlic cloves, peeled

2 tbsp extra virgin olive oil

4 garlic cloves, peeled and crushed

125 g/4 oz fresh mixed shellfish including their shells, e.g. mussels and clams

¼ tsp paprika

150 g/5 oz fresh or frozen shell-free scallops

150 g/5 oz fresh or frozen baby squid, cut into 1 cm/½ inch slices

sea salt

spring onion (scallion) ribbons, to garnish

Place any frozen seafood in the fridge to defrost overnight.

Bring a pan of salted water to the boil with the bay leaf and 2 cloves of garlic. Add the octopus tentacles, bring to the boil and then simmer gently with a lid on for 30–45 minutes until you can pierce the flesh with a fork. Take care not to overcook as it will become mushy. Once cooked, remove from the water and allow to cool.

In a medium pan, fry 1 tablespoon of the olive oil with 2 crushed garlic cloves over a medium heat for 2–3 minutes. Add 120 ml/4 fl oz/½ cup water and bring to the boil.

Reduce to a simmer, add the fresh mixed shellfish, cover and cook until all the shells have opened, about 3 minutes. Using a slotted spoon, transfer the shellfish to a large bowl and set aside, removing any unopened shells.

In a frying pan, heat the remaining tablespoon of olive oil over a medium heat. Add the remaining crushed garlic and the paprika and cook for 1 minute, stirring continuously. Add the octopus and prawns (jumbo shrimp) and cook for 4–5 minutes, stirring regularly, until the prawns are pink. Remove with a slotted spoon and add them to the bowl with the shellfish. Add the scallops to the frying pan. Cook for 3 minutes, turning over halfway through. Remove and add to the bowl of seafood. Finally, cook the squid for 1 minute, add to the seafood bowl and season everything with salt. Decant into a serving bowl, garnish with spring onion (scallion) and eat with crusty bread and olive oil.

SEARED SEA BASS ON TAGLIATELLE

With a dish this simple, it is important to focus on quality. It is all about the fresh flavours of delicious ingredients, and a dish like this really allows them to shine.

Serves 2

20 mixed cherry tomatoes, halved

extra virgin olive oil, for drizzling

sea salt and freshly ground black pepper

200 g/7 oz tagliatelle

2 sea bass steaks

1 tbsp fresh parsley and basil, finely chopped

Mix the cherry tomatoes with a drizzle of olive oil and a little salt and pepper to taste.

Bring a large pan of salted water to the boil and cook the tagliatelle according to the packet instructions.

While the pasta is cooking, heat a frying pan over a medium heat with a drizzle of olive oil in the bottom. Season the sea bass with salt and pepper and cook for 3–4 minutes, skin-side down. Gently turn the fish over and cook for a further minute.

Drain the pasta, toss with a drizzle of olive oil and a little salt. Divide between two plates, top with the sea bass and serve with the tomato salad. Finish with a sprinkle of chopped parsley and basil.

SIMPLE FISH & VEG EN PAPILLOTE

This simple and healthy dish uses deliciously aromatic green peppercorns. If you don't have green peppercorns, you can use black instead, although you will need fewer as black pepper has a stronger flavour.

Serves 2

½ tsp green peppercorns

2 salmon fillets

¼ lemon

sea salt

1 medium courgette (zucchini)

10 cherry tomatoes, halved

extra virgin olive oil for drizzling

fresh thyme to garnish (optional)

Preheat the oven to 190°C/375°F/Gas Mark 5.

Reserve a few peppercorns for garnishing and crush or grind the rest.

Put each salmon fillet on a large square of baking parchment, squeeze over the lemon and season with salt and ground green pepper to taste.

Top and tail the courgette (zucchini). Using a peeler, slice the courgette into fine ribbons along its length.

Place a couple of squares of fresh baking parchment into two bowls. Arrange the courgette ribbons on the paper. Season with salt and a little of the crushed green peppercorns.

Remove the salmon from the baking parchment and place on top of the courgette. Scatter over the cherry tomatoes. Drizzle the whole dish with olive oil. Garnish with the whole peppercorns and fresh thyme. Serve as a light lunch or eat with simple pasta or potatoes for a heartier dish.

SICILIAN SARDINE PASTA

Make this dish with fresh or canned sardines. Of course, fresh is always best, but it is often easier using precooked fish. Be aware that precooked sardines will fall apart more than fresh sardines in the pasta dish.

Serves 4

For the fennel pesto

1 head fresh fennel, roughly chopped

2 tbsp parsley

65 g/2½ oz/½ cup pine nuts

50 g/2 oz/⅓ cup freshly grated parmesan cheese

3 garlic cloves, peeled, crushed or minced (chopped)

6 tbsp extra virgin olive oil

sea salt and freshly ground black pepper

For the pasta

bucatini pasta or spaghetti

drizzle extra virgin olive oil

fresh sardine fillets or canned sardines

sultanas (golden raisins)

To make the pesto, blitz all the pesto ingredients in a food processor. Season with salt and pepper to taste.

Bring a large pan of salted water to the boil and cook the pasta according to the packet instructions.

If using fresh sardines, heat a drizzle of olive oil in a frying pan over a medium heat. Cook the sardines for 2 minutes on each side or until just cooked and still holding their shape. If using canned sardines, drain them ready for use. Drain the pasta and toss thoroughly with the fennel pesto and sultanas (golden raisins).

If using fresh sardines, gently mix them in now. If using precooked sardines, wait until the pasta is dished up and place the fillets on top of the pasta. Serve as it is or with crusty bread and a green salad.

POTATO BOULANGÈRE
with Grilled Fish

Boulangère is a classic French dish. I have used perch in this recipe, but if you can't get hold of perch, it also works beautifully with pollock or cod.

Serves 2

1 tbsp extra virgin olive oil, plus more for drizzling

1 small red onion, finely sliced

2 garlic cloves, peeled and crushed

1 tbsp rosemary leaves

4 slices serrano ham, chopped

450 g/1 lb potatoes, peeled and thinly sliced

salt and freshly ground black pepper

300 ml/½ pint/1¼ cups vegetable stock

350 g/12 oz perch fillets

For the garnish

few chives

1 lemon wedge

1 slice serrano ham

Preheat the oven to 190°C/375°F/Gas Mark 5.

Heat 1 tablespoon of olive oil in a frying pan over a medium heat. Add the onion and cook for 5 minutes, stirring regularly. Add the garlic and the rosemary and cook for a further minute. Remove the pan from the heat and stir in the serrano ham.

Lightly grease a shallow 1.4 litre/2/½ pint/1½ quart baking dish with olive oil. Layer the potato slices and onion mix alternately in the prepared dish, seasoning each layer with salt and pepper.

Pour the stock over the top, then drizzle with olive oil. Bake in the preheated oven for 60–70 minutes. Check after 50–60 minutes and cover with kitchen foil when nicely browned.

Lightly rinse the perch fillets and pat dry on absorbent paper towels. Cook on a griddle, or shallow fry in a little olive oil for 3–4 minutes on each side. Remove from the pan with a slotted spatula and drain on absorbent paper towels.

Remove the potatoes from the oven and place the fish on the top. Garnish with snipped chives, a slice of serrano ham and a wedge of lemon and serve immediately.

PARMA-HAM-WRAPPED COD

Italians love to wrap fish and chicken in ham. This delicious combination of cod and Parma ham is no exception and the saltiness of the ham marries beautifully with the sweet subtlety of the cod.

Serves 4

1 tsp dried oregano

pinch sea salt

4 x 175 g/6 oz thick cod fillets

4 slices Parma ham

12 baby asparagus

12 baby corn, halved lengthways

1 tbsp extra virgin olive oil

2 tbsp lemon juice

sea salt and freshly ground black pepper

Preheat the oven to 200°C/400°F/Gas Mark 6.

Sprinkle the dried oregano and a pinch of salt over the cod fillets. Wrap each cod fillet in a slice of Parma ham and put to one side.

Toss the asparagus and corn in the olive oil and lemon juice. Season with salt and pepper and place in a baking tray. Add the wrapped cod fillets and cook in the oven for 15–20 minutes until the fish is cooked through. Serve immediately.

MUSSELS LINGUINE

A flatter variety of pasta, linguine is popularly served with light-textured sauces and seafood, such as in this classic Italian dish.

Serves 4

For the sauce

2 tbsp extra virgin olive oil

1 small onion, peeled and finely diced

2 garlic cloves, peeled and crushed

small pinch chili flakes

200 g/7 oz/1 cups fresh tomatoes,
   peeled and finely chopped

large pinch sea salt

225 g/8 oz dried linguine or tagliatelle

For the mussels

1 tbsp extra virgin olive oil

1 onion, peeled and finely chopped

300 ml/½ pint/1¼ cups medium dry white wine

2 kg/4½ lb fresh mussels, washed and scrubbed

2 tbsp freshly chopped parsley

To make the sauce, heat the olive oil in a medium-size saucepan and gently fry the onion for 5–7 minutes until soft and transparent. Add the garlic and chili flakes and cook for another minute, stirring continually. Add the tomatoes and salt. Bring to the boil and simmer for 7–10 minutes until the sauce begins to thicken. Keep warm while you cook the rest of the dish.

Bring a large pan of salted water to the boil and cook the pasta according to the packet instructions. Once cooked, drain, toss in a little olive oil and put a lid on the pan to keep warm.

For the mussels, add the olive oil, onion and wine to a large pan. Bring to the boil, add the mussels and cover with a close-fitting lid. Steam for 5–6 minutes, shaking the pan gently to ensure even cooking. Discard any mussels that have not opened, then strain the liquor. Stir 4 tablespoons of the liquor into the tomato sauce.

Toss the sauce and pasta together. Gently mix in the mussels. Sprinkle with chopped parsley (and more chili flakes if you like extra heat) and serve immediately.

PAELLA

Originally from Valencia, paella became known as Spain's national dish, although the Spanish consider it still to be a regional dish. Paella is traditionally a feast recipe for special occasions.

Serves 6

4 tbsp extra virgin olive oil

6 chicken legs

1 onion, peeled and finely chopped

2 garlic cloves, peeled and crushed

225 g/8 oz/¾ cup tomatoes, skinned, deseeded and chopped

2 red peppers, deseeded and chopped

1 tsp paprika

450 g/1 lb/2¼ cups Arborio rice

½ tsp turmeric

900 ml/1½ pints/3¾ cups chicken stock, warmed

300 g/11 oz white fish, such as cod or haddock

175 g/6 oz/1 cup large raw prawns (jumbo shrimp), tails on

125 g/4½ oz/⅔ cup frozen peas

450 g/1 lb fresh mussels including shells, rinsed and cleaned

salt and freshly ground black pepper

juice of 1 lime

1 lemon, cut into wedges

Heat the olive oil in a paella pan or large heavy-based frying pan. Cook the chicken legs for 10–15 minutes until golden. Remove and keep warm.

Add the onion and garlic to the pan and fry for 2–3 minutes. Add the tomatoes, peppers and paprika, cooking for a further 3 minutes. Add the rice, cooked chicken, turmeric and half the stock. Bring to the boil and simmer, gradually adding more stock as it is absorbed. Cook for 20 minutes, or until most of the stock has been absorbed and the rice is almost tender.

Steam the fish for 6–8 minutes until cooked and just falling apart. Keep warm. While the fish is cooking, fry the prawns (jumbo shrimp) in a little olive oil, salt and pepper over a medium heat, until they turn nicely pink. Keep warm.

Stir the peas into the paella and heat through for 3–5 minutes.

Put the mussels in a large saucepan with 5 cm/2 inches boiling salted water. Cover and steam for 5 minutes. Discard any with unopened shells.

Squeeze the lime juice over the paella. Scatter over the fish, prawns and mussels. Arrange the lemon on top of the paella and serve immediately.

SEAFOOD RISOTTO

Italian Arborio rice is a short-grain rice variety that grows in the Po Valley and is excellent in all risotto dishes. Traditionally, risotto requires continual stirring during cooking, but the method I have used here is easier.

Serves 4

50 g/2 oz/4 tbsp butter

2 shallots, peeled and finely chopped

1 garlic clove, peeled and crushed

350 g/12 oz/1⅔ cups Arborio rice

150 ml/¼ pint/⅔ cup white wine

600 ml/1 pint/2½ cups fish
   or vegetable stock, heated

2 tsp extra virgin olive oil

8 mushrooms, sliced

16 baby asparagus, cut in half

125 g/4½ oz/¾ cup prawns
   (shrimp), tails on

freshly grated Parmesan
   cheese, to serve

Melt the butter in a large heavy-based saucepan, add the shallots and garlic and cook for 2 minutes until slightly softened. Add the rice and cook for 1–2 minutes, stirring continuously, then pour in the wine and boil for 1 minute. Pour in half the hot stock, bring to the boil, cover the saucepan and simmer gently for 15 minutes, adding the remaining stock a little at a time. Continue to simmer for 5 minutes, or until the rice is cooked and all the liquid is absorbed.

Meanwhile, heat the olive oil in a frying pan and fry the mushrooms over a medium heat for 5 minutes, stirring regularly. Set aside and keep warm.

Steam or boil the asparagus for 5–7 minutes until just cooked.

When the rice has cooked, stir in the prawns (shrimp), then heat through until the prawns are pink and everything is piping hot. Serve in bowls, with the mushrooms and asparagus scattered on top. Grate on some Parmesan cheese and serve immediately.

BACCALÀ ALLA LIVORNESE

Baccalà, salt cod, is available from Italian delicatessens, select fishmongers and larger supermarkets. You will need to soak the salt cod in this recipe 2–3 days ahead. It's well worth the wait!

Serves 6

500 g/1 lb 2 oz baccalà (salt cod) fillet, skin and bones removed

120 ml/4 fl oz/½ cup olive oil

2 large onions, peeled and thinly sliced

1 garlic clove, peeled and finely chopped

4 anchovy fillets

1 tbsp capers

1 small red chili, finely chopped

3 fresh bay leaves

1 tsp basil pesto

400 g/14 oz/1⅔ cups canned chopped tomatoes

250 ml/8 fl oz/1 cup white wine

sea salt and freshly ground black pepper

1 large caper berry to garnish (optional)

Place the baccalà (salt cod) in a large bowl and cover with cold water. Refrigerate for 2–3 days, changing the water four times to remove the salt. Drain, cut into 6 pieces and set aside.

Preheat the oven to 180°C/350°F/Gas Mark 4.

Heat oil in a large saucepan over a medium heat. Add the onions and garlic and sauté for 7–10 minutes until translucent. Stir in the anchovies, capers, chili, bay leaves, pesto and tomatoes and cook for 7 minutes, stirring regularly. Add the wine, bring to the boil and simmer for 5 minutes. Taste and season with salt, if necessary, and pepper.

Place the baccalà in a baking dish, pour over the sauce, cover in foil and bake for 20–30 minutes until the fish is cooked. Garnish with a caper berry (if using) and serve with crusty bread and a green salad.

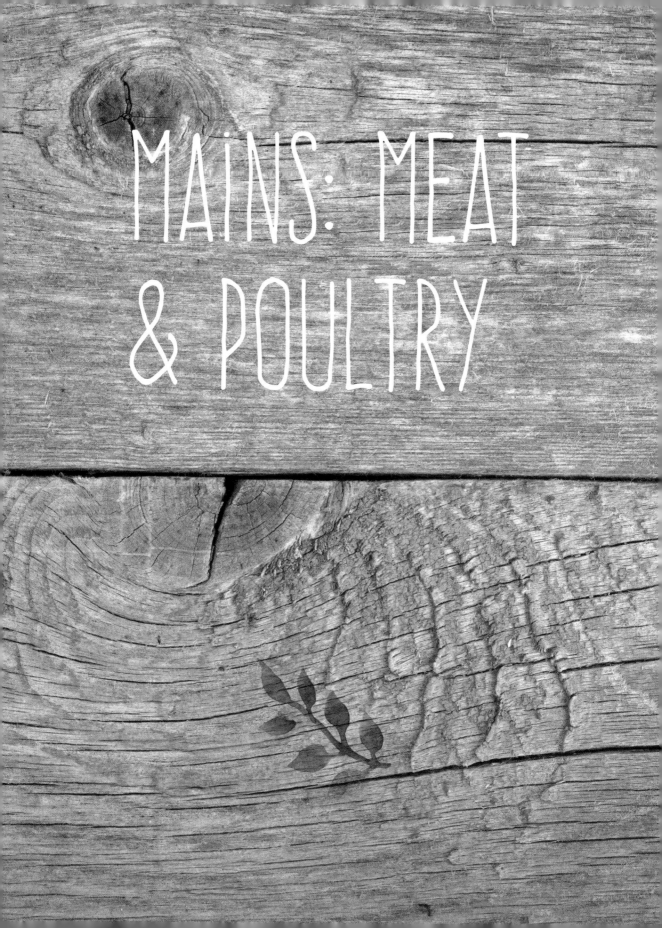

MAINS: MEAT & POULTRY

MOUSSAKA

Moussaka is real comfort food. As this version is a low in carbs, you will still feel clean and energised after eating it. It is also a great dish for weight loss or weight maintenance.

Serves 6

4 medium aubergines (eggplants), cut into 5 mm (¼-inch) rounds

8 tbsp olive oil

800 g/28 oz lamb mince (ground lamb)

1 onion, peeled and finely chopped

3 garlic cloves, peeled and crushed

4 tsp dried oregano

2 bay leaves

whole nutmeg, for grating

400 g/14 oz/1⅔ cups canned chopped tomatoes

2 tbsp tomato paste

400 ml/14 fl oz/1⅔ cups water

sea salt and freshly ground black pepper

For the béchamel sauce

10 g/¼ oz/½ tbsp butter

10 g/1⁄3 oz/4 tsp plain/all-purpose flour

120 ml/4 fl oz/½ cup whole milk or oat milk

10 g/1/4 oz/1 tbsp Parmesan cheese, finely grated (optional)

sea salt and freshly ground black pepper

40 g/1½ oz/3½ tbsp Parmesan, coarsely grated

Over a high heat, fry the slices of aubergine (eggplant) in 6 tablespoons of olive oil in batches for 5–7 mins until golden. Set aside on a plate lined with paper towels.

Heat 1 tablespoon of olive oil in a frying pan over a medium-high heat. Add the mince (ground lamb) and fry for 8–10 minutes until browned, stirring regularly to break up any lumps. Tip the mince into a bowl and set aside. Add the final tablespoon of oil to the pan. Fry the onion gently for 10–12 minutes until soft and translucent. Add the garlic, oregano, bay leaves and a fine grating of nutmeg and cook for another minute. Add the mince to the pan with the tomatoes, tomato paste and water. Season with salt and pepper. Bring to the boil, lower the heat and simmer uncovered for 25 minutes, stirring occasionally, until the sauce has thickened. Add a little more water if necessary.

Heat the oven to 200C°/390F°/Gas Mark 4.

In a small pan, melt the butter over a medium heat. Stir in the flour and cook for 1 minute. Remove the pan from the heat. Whisk in the milk little by little to make a smooth sauce. Return to the heat and, stirring continuously, bring to a simmer. Cook for 3 minutes. Turn off the heat and whisk in the finely grated Parmesan. Season with salt and pepper to taste.

In a large baking dish, spread out one third of the mince. Add a layer of aubergine followed by the rest of the meat and another layer of aubergine. Finish with the béchamel sauce, spreading it out evenly. Finish by sprinkling over the coarsely grated Parmesan.

Place in the oven and cook for 40–50 minutes until golden on top.

SPICY CHICKEN & MANGO SKEWERS
with Herby Bulgur Wheat

Used in Turkish, Greek and Albanian recipes, bulgur wheat is made from wholewheat grains. It has a light, nutty flavour that works really well with fresh herbs.

Serves 4

400 g/14 oz chicken breast fillet

1 mango, halved, pitted and peeled

50 ml/2 fl oz/¼ cup yogurt

1 tbsp extra virgin olive oil

1 garlic clove, peeled and crushed

1 small red chili, deseeded and finely chopped

finely grated zest and juice of ½ lemon

sea salt and freshly ground black pepper

fresh parsley sprigs, to garnish

For the herby bulgur wheat

175 g/6 oz/1 cup bulgur wheat

1 tsp olive oil

juice of ½ lemon

2 tbsp parsley, freshly chopped

2 tbsp mint, freshly shredded

sea salt and freshly ground black pepper

If using wooden skewers, presoak them in cold water for at least 30 minutes. (This stops them from burning during grilling (broiling).) Cut the chicken and the mango into bite-size chunks and place in a shallow dish.

Mix together the yogurt, olive oil, garlic, chili, lemon zest and juice. Season with salt and pepper. Pour over the chicken and mango and toss to coat. Cover and leave to marinate in the refrigerator for up to 8 hours.

Put the bulgur wheat in a bowl. Pour over enough boiling water to cover. Put a plate over the bowl. Leave to soak for 20 minutes.

For the dressing, whisk together the oil and lemon juice in a bowl.

Drain the bulgur wheat and squeeze out any excess moisture in a clean dish towel. Combine with the dressing and herbs and season to taste with salt and pepper.

Thread the chicken strips onto 8 wooden or metal skewers. Cook under a hot grill (broiler) for 8 minutes. Turn halfway through until the chicken is lightly browned and cooked through. Spoon the herby bulgur wheat onto individual plates. Arrange the chicken skewers on top and garnish with the parsley sprigs. Serve warm.

CHICKEN CHASSEUR

French in origin, this recipe is used throughout many Mediterranean coastal regions, although each may have its own variation. Serve with a crusty French loaf and plenty of butter.

Serves 4-8

2 tbsp extra virgin olive oil

15 g/½ oz/1 tbsp butter

8 chicken thighs

1 large red onion, peeled and diced

1 small red pepper, deseeded and diced

3 garlic cloves, peeled and sliced

175 g/6 oz/1¾ cups mushrooms, wiped clean

2 tbsp plain (all-purpose) flour

150 ml/¼ pint/⅔ cup dry white wine

400g/14 oz/1⅔ cups canned
    chopped tomatoes

2 tbsp tomato paste

350 ml/12 fl oz/1½ cups chicken stock

2 tarragon sprigs

salt and freshly ground black pepper

1 tsp freshly chopped tarragon, to garnish

Preheat the oven to 180°C/350°F/Gas Mark 4.

Heat the oil and butter in an ovenproof casserole dish, add the chicken portions and cook, in batches if necessary, until browned on both sides. Remove with a slotted spoon and reserve.

Add the onion and red pepper to the casserole dish and cook for 5 minutes. Add the garlic and cook for another minute. Cut the mushrooms in half if large, then add to the casserole dish and cook for 2 minutes. Sprinkle in the flour and cook for 2 minutes. Remove from the heat and stir in the wine. Put back on the heat, adding the chopped tomatoes, tomato paste and stock. Stir thoroughly, add the tarragon sprigs and bring to the boil, stirring constantly.

Return the chicken to the casserole dish, season to taste, cover with a lid and cook in the oven for 45–50 minutes until the chicken is cooked. Serve sprinkled with chopped tarragon.

MOROCCAN LAMB WITH APRICOTS

The use of warming cardamom, ginger and cumin make this a mouth-wateringly aromatic dish while it is slowly cooking. Fill your kitchen with the smell of deliciousness!

Serves 6

2 tbsp olive oil

450 g/1 lb lamb neck fillet, cubed

1 large red onion, peeled and chopped

5 cm/2 inch piece root ginger
   (fresh ginger), peeled and grated

3 garlic cloves, peeled and crushed

1 tsp ground cardamom

1 tsp ground cumin

1 cinnamon stick

¼–½ tsp chili/pepper flakes

400 g/14 oz/1⅔ cups canned
   chopped tomatoes

400 ml/14 fl oz/1⅔ cups lamb or
   vegetable stock

125 g/4 oz unsulphured dried apricots

400 g/14 oz canned chickpeas
   (garbanzos), drained

3 tbsp shelled pistachios, crushed

fresh coriander (cilantro), to garnish

giant (pearl/Israeli) couscous, to serve

Add 1 tablespoon of olive oil to a frying pan over a high heat. Fry the lamb in batches for about 5 minutes until golden brown. Remove the lamb from the pan and set aside. Reduce the heat, add another tablespoon of olive oil to the pan and fry the onion for 5 minutes. Add the ginger, garlic and dried spices and cook for another 2 minutes. Add the lamb back in and continue cooking for 10 minutes, stirring regularly.

Add the chopped tomatoes and stock, cover and simmer for 60 minutes, stirring from time to time. Add the apricots and chickpeas (garbanzos) and simmer for a further 15 minutes.

Garnish with the crushed pistachios and coriander (cilantro) and serve with giant couscous.

CHERRY TOMATO & CHICKEN
Farfalle

This simple pasta dish is a winner with adults and children alike. There is nothing fancy about it, and yet the fresh flavours still make it something to write home about.

Serves 4

2 tbsp extra virgin olive oil

2 large chicken breasts

sea salt and freshly ground black pepper

2 garlic cloves, crushed or minced (finely chopped)

¼ tsp smoked paprika

400g/14 oz/1⅔ cups canned chopped tomatoes

20 cherry tomatoes, halved

350 g/12 oz farfalle pasta

1 small bunch basil, to garnish

Heat the oil in a frying pan over a medium heat. Season the chicken breasts with salt and pepper and add to the frying pan. Turn down the heat and cook with the lid on for 20 minutes until cooked through, turning the chicken breasts over halfway through. Remove from the pan and, once cool enough to handle, cut into bite-size pieces. Reserve the juices in the frying pan to make the sauce.

Add the garlic and smoked paprika to the frying pan and cook over a low heat for 2 minutes, stirring continually. Add the chopped tomatoes and cherry tomatoes. Bring to the boil, reduce to a simmer and cook with the lid off for 10 minutes until the cherry tomatoes are softening and the sauce thickens. Stir in the cooked chicken pieces and bring back to the boil for a few minutes to heat the chicken through.

While the sauce is cooking, bring a large pan of salted water to the boil and cook the farfalle according to the packet instructions. Once cooked, drain and put a lid on the pan to keep warm whilst you finish the sauce.

Stir the sauce through the pasta and serve immediately, topped with fresh basil leaves.

OVEN-BAKED CHICKEN
with Potato Wedges

This is a lovely variation on a Sunday roast that is simple enough to serve any day of the week. Have fun experimenting with different spices and herbs if you want to get creative with this dish.

Serves 6

For the chicken

2 tsp honey

1 tsp paprika

½ lemon, juice and zest

1 tbsp coriander seeds

3 tbsp extra virgin olive oil

¼ tsp sea salt

freshly ground black pepper

6 pieces chicken, drumsticks and thighs

For the potatoes

2 medium waxy potatoes, cut into wedges

2 tbsp extra virgin olive oil

2 fresh rosemary sprigs

2 fresh thyme sprigs

pinch sea salt

6 garlic cloves, skins on

Preheat the oven to 200°C/400°F/Gas Mark 6.

In a baking pan, mix together the honey, paprika, lemon juice, coriander seeds, olive oil and salt. Season with black pepper. Add the chicken and coat in the marinade. Set aside while you prepare the potatoes.

In a separate baking pan, toss the potato wedges with the olive oil. Strip the leaves off one rosemary sprig and one thyme sprig and stir into the potatoes. Season with salt.

Put the tray of chicken and the tray of potatoes in the oven to cook for 40 minutes in total. After 25 minutes stir the potatoes and scatter over the garlic cloves.

Continue to bake until the chicken and potatoes are beginning to brown and are cooked through.

Strip the remaining rosemary and thyme leaves. Arrange the chicken and potatoes in a serving dish and scatter over the stripped herbs just before serving.

CHICKEN PICCATA

This sophisticated chicken dish is actually very simple to make. I love chicken piccata served with buttery mashed potatoes and a green salad.

Serves 2-4

2 large skinless chicken breasts

65 g/2½ oz/½ cup plain (all-purpose) flour

¼ teaspoon salt

pinch freshly ground black pepper

15 g/½ oz/4 tsp finely grated
   Parmesan cheese

2 tbsp extra virgin olive oil

40 g/1½ oz/3 tbsp butter

120 ml/4 fl oz/½ cup chicken stock

120 ml/4 fl oz/½ cup dry white wine
   or more chicken stock

2 tbsp lemon juice

4 tbsp capers

sea salt and freshly ground
   black pepper

basil leaves to garnish (optional)

Slice the chicken breasts in half horizontally.

Mix together the flour, salt, pepper and Parmesan. Wet the chicken breasts with water and coat them in the flour mix.

Heat the olive oil and 2 tablespoons of the butter in a large frying pan over a medium-high heat. Add the chicken and fry for 3 minutes each side until lightly browned. Remove the chicken from the pan and keep warm in the oven.

Add the chicken stock, white wine, lemon juice and capers to the frying pan and bring to the boil, scraping any bits off the bottom of the pan. Reduce the sauce by half. Whisk in the butter. Season with salt and pepper to taste.

Serve the chicken with the sauce poured over the top and garnish with basil leaves, if liked.

HERBY LAMB & YOGURT PITAS

These lamb patties are so good! The combination of dried and fresh herbs and spices makes them mouth-wateringly flavoursome and they work beautifully with the freshness of yogurt.

Serves 3-4

For the patties

300 g/11 oz lamb mince (ground lamb)

3 spring onions (scallions), finely sliced

3 garlic cloves, peeled and crushed

1 tsp ground cumin

2 tsp ground coriander

¾ tsp sea salt

freshly ground black pepper

1 tbsp fresh mint, finely chopped

1 tbsp fresh coriander, finely chopped

1 egg

drizzle extra virgin olive oil or sunflower oil

For the kebabs

3–4 pita breads

½ red onion, peeled and finely sliced

1 tomato, finely sliced

¼ fresh red chili, finely sliced

fresh coriander (cilantro), to garnish

6 tbsp full-fat plain yogurt

In a mixing bowl, thoroughly combine all the ingredients for the patties. With clean wet hands, shape the mixture into 3–4 equal round patties.

Heat a non-stick frying pan over a medium-high heat. When the oil is hot add the patties and fry for 5–7 minutes on each side until nicely browned.

Cut the pita breads in half and stuff with the patties, red onion, tomato, red chilli, some fresh coriander (cilantro) leaves and a spoonful of yogurt. Serve while the patties are still warm.

PORK SHISH SKEWERS

These tasty kebabs can be barbequed for that summer feeling or cooked under the grill (broiler) for a quick supper or fun lunch with friends at any time of year.

Makes 8 skewers

1 tsp coriander seeds

½ tsp cumin seeds

½ tsp black peppercorns

¼ tsp ground cinnamon

1 tsp sea salt

3 tbsp extra virgin olive oil

1 tbsp lemon juice

4 pork steaks

2 peppers (e.g. yellow and green)

1 medium white onion, peeled

new potatoes and ratatouille, to serve

(*see* page 141)

Toast the coriander and cumin seeds over a medium heat for 1–2 minutes, shaking the pan continuously until the spices smell aromatic.

In a pestle and mortar or spice grinder, grind the toasted seeds with the peppercorns, cinnamon and salt. Add the ground spices to a large mixing bowl with the olive oil and lemon juice. Mix into a paste.

Cut the pork steaks, peppers and onion into generous bite-size pieces for the skewers. Add the pork and peppers to the marinating paste. Mix until thoroughly coated. Leave to stand in the fridge for at least 30 minutes, or overnight.

If using wooden skewers, presoak them in cold water for at least 30 minutes. (This stops them from burning during grilling (broiling).)

Thread the pork and vegetables onto eight skewers, alternating ingredients. Cook on the barbeque or under a hot grill (broiler) for 10–12 until just beginning to char. Serve hot with ratatouille and buttery new potatoes.

BREADED PORK
with Panzanella

Panzanella is a Tuscan salad, and a delicious way to use up good-quality leftover bread, although fresh bread works in this recipe too. It goes well with breaded pork in this recipe.

Serves 4

For the panzanella

200 g/7 oz stale white crusty bread

5 tbsp extra virgin olive oil

1 small red onion, peeled and finely diced

3 medium tomatoes, deseeded and finely diced

50 g/2 oz/½ cup pine nuts, toasted

small bunch fresh parsley, chopped

1 tbsp white wine vinegar

1 anchovy, finely chopped

1 small garlic clove, peeled and crushed

½ tsp dried oregano

sea salt and freshly ground black pepper

For the breaded pork

2 tbsp plain (all-purpose) flour

1 egg, beaten

100 g/3½ oz/1½ cups fresh
   white breadcrumbs

25 g/1 oz/2 tbsp Parmesan
   cheese, grated

freshly ground pepper

4 pork loin steaks

drizzle extra virgin olive oil

Preheat the oven to 190°C/375°F/Gas Mark 5.

To make the breaded pork, sprinkle the flour onto a side plate. Pour the beaten egg onto a second plate. On a third plate, combine the breadcrumbs and Parmesan and season with black pepper. Dip the pork chops in the flour, coating completely. Next dip them into the egg, before finally coating them in breadcrumbs.

Grease a baking pan with a drizzle of olive oil. Place the breaded pork on the tray and bake in the oven for 30–40 minutes, until the breadcrumbs are lightly browned and the chops are fully cooked.

To make the panzanella, cut the bread into 1 cm/½ inch cubes. Toss with 2 tbsp olive oil. Scatter over a baking pan and bake in the oven for 10–12 minutes until lightly golden.

Add the toasted bread to a bowl with the red onion, tomatoes, pine nuts and parsley.

Whisk together the remaining olive oil with the vinegar, chopped anchovy, crushed garlic and dried oregano. Season the dressing to taste and toss with the bread salad. Serve together with the breaded pork.

TREATS & DESSERTS

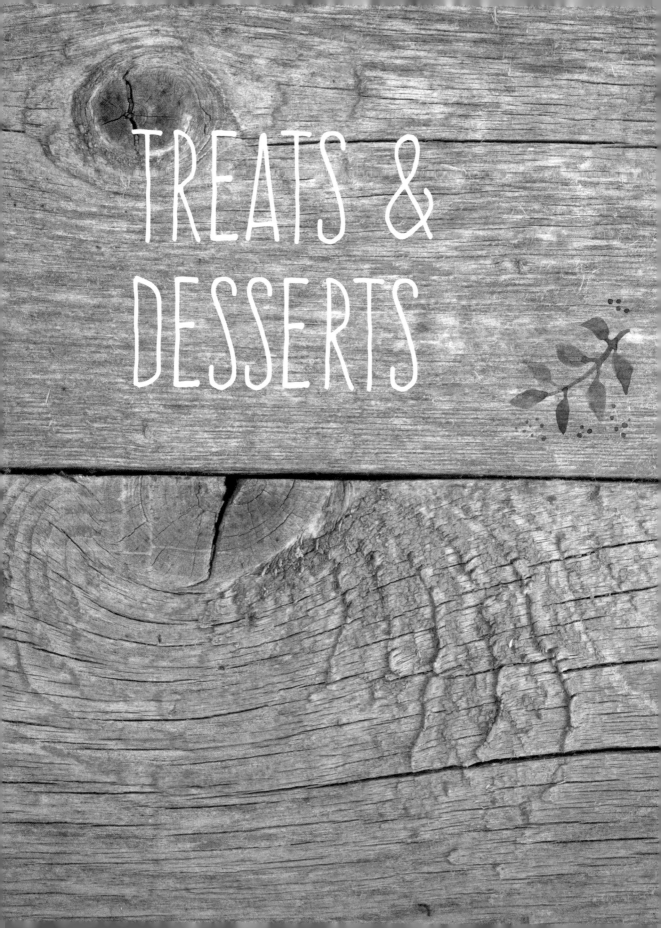

FLOURLESS CHOCOLATE ORANGE CAKE

This is such an easy and delicious cake to make. I bring it out for special occasions or, if I am feeling extravagant, double the recipe and make a traybake (sheet cake). It freezes well.

Serves 8–10

2 blood oranges or small normal oranges

6 large (jumbo) eggs

1½ tsp baking powder

½ tsp baking soda

165 g/5¾ oz/¾ cup sugar

200 g/7 oz/2 cups ground almonds

100 g/3½ oz/¾ cup unsweetened cocoa powder

1 tsp ground cinnamon

pinch salt

Greek yogurt or whipped cream, to serve

Submerge the whole oranges in a pan of boiling water and simmer for 1 hour until soft, topping up with water if necessary. Once cooked, remove from the pan and allow to cool. Once cooled, cut open and remove any pips (seeds).

Preheat the oven to 180°C/350°F/Gas Mark 4. Grease a 20 cm/8-inch cake pan with butter and line with baking parchment.

Add the orange to a blender and blend until smooth. Add the rest of the ingredients and blend again until just smooth. Do not over-blend.

Pour the cake batter into the cake pan, spreading it out evenly. Bake for 40–60 minutes.

Check the cake after 40 minutes. When it is baked, it will be set and a knife inserted into the middle will come out clean. If it needs longer, cover in baking parchment to prevent it burning on top. Once cooked, remove from the oven and allow to cool in the pan.

Delicious served with Greek yogurt or whipped cream.

APRICOT TARTE TATIN

French tart tatin is a traditional dish made with fresh fruit, most often apples. In this summer variation take advantage of seasonal fresh apricots to create a stunning dessert.

Serves 4-6

50 g/2 oz/¼ cup golden caster (unbleached superfine) sugar
500 g/1 lb 2 oz ripe fresh apricots
50 g/2 oz/4 tbsp salted butter
500 g/1 lb 2 oz all-butter puff pastry
cream or yogurt, to serve

Put the sugar into a 20 cm/8 inch heavy-based ovenproof frying pan or tatin pan with 1 tablespoon of water. Leave to sit while you prepare the apricots: cut each apricot in half and remove the pit. Set aside.

Cook the sugar and water mix over a medium heat for 3–5 minutes until golden and sticky. Remove from the heat and stir the butter in well. Arrange the apricots cut-side up in the pan, being careful not to burn yourself on the hot caramel. Put back onto the heat and cook for 5 minutes. Remove from the heat and leave to cool completely.

Preheat the oven to 200°C/400°F/Gas Mark 6.

Roll out the pastry slightly larger than the pan with the apricots. Place the pastry on top of the pan and tuck the edges in around the fruit. Bake for 35 minutes until the pastry is golden. Remove from the oven and allow to cool slightly.

To turn the tart out, wear oven gloves, place a plate on top of the pan and flip the plate and pan over together in one movement, being very careful of the hot caramel. Serve warm with cream or yogurt.

HONEY BAKLAVA

Making your own baklava is surprisingly easy and tastes so good! I have used pistachios, almonds and pecans in this recipe, but feel free to substitute other nuts if you have them.

Makes around 24 pieces

200 g/7 oz/¾ cup plus 2 tbsp butter, plus extra for greasing

200 g/7 oz/1½ cups pistachios

50 g/1¾ oz/⅓ cup almonds

50 g/2 oz/½ cup pecans

3 tbsp honey

pinch sea salt

350 g/12 oz filo (phyllo) pastry

For the syrup

250 g/9 oz/1¼ cups golden caster (unbeached supefine) sugar

50 g/2 oz/2½ tbsp honey

2 tsp orange blossom water

½ tsp ground cinnamon

¼ tsp ground cardamom (from 3 pods)

200 ml/7 fl oz/¾ cup water

Heat the oven to 180°C/350°F/Gas Mark 4.

Grease a 20 x 20 cm/8 x 8-inch square cake pan with butter. Using a food processor, pulse the nuts into small pieces. Stir in the honey with a pinch of salt.

Over a low heat, melt the butter. Cut the filo (phyllo) pastry sheets in half. Trim to fit the pan. Divide the sheets in two and cover one half with a damp dish towel to stop them drying out. Layer the filo in the tin, brushing each layer with melted butter until the first pile of filo sheets is finished.

Next, spoon the nut mixture into the cake tin. Flatten it down gently with the back of a spoon. Using the second pile of filo, add more layers, brushing with butter. Drizzle any remaining butter over the last filo sheet. With a sharp knife, cut through the pastry to create square or diamond shapes.

Bake in the oven for 20 mins. Reduce the heat to 150°C/300°F/Gas Mark 2 and bake for another 45 mins.

Combine all the syrup ingredients in a pan. Over a low heat, dissolve the sugar. Bring to a boil for 8–10 minutes until syrupy. When the baklava is cooked, drizzle evenly with warm syrup. Leave to cool completely before serving.

GOATS' CHEESE & LEMON TART

This tasty, tangy tart is a twist on the traditional French lemon tart. It can be a sophisticated dinner party dessert or an exciting offering for friends coming over for coffee.

Serves 4

For the pastry

125 g/4½ oz/1 stick cold butter, cut into small pieces

225 g/8 oz/1¾ cups plain (all-purpose) flour

pinch salt

50 g/2 oz/4 tbsp granulated sugar

1 medium (large) egg yolk

For the filling

350 g/12 oz/1½ cups mild fresh soft goats' cheese

3 egg yolks, beaten

150 g/5 oz/¾ cup granulated sugar

grated zest and juice of 3 lemons

450 ml/¾ pint/2 cups double (heavy) cream

icing (confectioners') sugar

Rub the butter into the plain (all-purpose) flour and salt until the mixture resembles breadcrumbs. Stir in the sugar. Beat the egg yolk with 2 tablespoons cold water. Mix into the flour and butter with a butter knife to form a dough. Turn the dough out onto a lightly floured surface and knead until smooth. Chill in the refrigerator for 30 minutes.

Preheat the oven to 200°C/400°F/Gas Mark 6.

On a lightly floured surface, roll out the dough and line a 4 cm/1½ inch deep x 23 cm/9 inch wide fluted flan pan with it. Chill in the refrigerator for 10 minutes, then bake the pastry case blind for 10 minutes. Remove the blind baking beans or foil and return to the oven for a further 12–15 minutes until cooked. Remove the pan from the oven to cool.

Reduce the oven temperature to 150°C/300°F/Gas Mark 2.

Beat the goats' cheese with the egg yolks, sugar, lemon zest and juice. Mix in the cream. Pour the cheese mixture into the pastry case (shell) and return to the oven. Bake covered in baking parchment for 35–40 minutes, until just set. Chill in the refrigerator.

Sift over icing (confectioners') sugar just before serving.

GRIDDLED PEACHES
with Thyme & Honey

This simple dish is perfect for a dinner party. Get everything ready before your guests arrive, and then cook the peaches after the main course while everyone is chatting and digesting, ready for dessert.

Serves 6

6 ripe peaches
15 g/½ oz/1 tbsp butter
2 tbsp honey, plus extra to serve
small bunch lemon thyme
yogurt or cream, to serve

Slice the peaches in half and remove the pits.

Melt the butter and honey together with half the thyme sprigs. Simmer gently for 3 minutes, taking care not to burn the butter.

Brush the honey butter over the peaches and place in a ridged griddle pan over a medium heat. Cook the peach halves for 10 minutes until soft and slightly charred, turning over halfway through.

Serve hot with yogurt or cream, a drizzle of honey and a few fresh thyme sprigs.

STRAWBERRY GALETTES

This beautiful dessert is the perfect summer treat. Strawberry galettes are also delicious served up with a dollop of whipped cream and a nice cup of tea or coffee or homemade lemonade.

Makes 6

400 g/14 oz/2 cups fresh
   strawberries (sliced or cut into quarters)
50 g/2 oz/4 tbsp granulated sugar,
   plus extra for sprinkling
1 tsp vanilla extract

small pinch freshly ground black pepper
325 g/11½ oz all-butter puff pastry
1 egg, beaten
1 tsp icing (confectioners') sugar

Preheat the oven to 180°C/350°F/Gas Mark 4. Line a baking tray (sheet) with baking parchment.

In a bowl, combine the strawberries, sugar, vanilla extract and pepper and set to one side.

Divide the pastry into 6 equal portions. Lightly roll the pastry portions into balls between your palms. Flatten each ball with the palm of your hand and roll out to a circle roughly 14 cm/5½ inches across. Transfer to the baking tray.

With a slotted spoon, remove the strawberries from their juice and place in the centre of each pastry circle, leaving about 2 cm/¾ inch border around the edge. Gently fold and pinch the edges of the pastry up to create a bowl to contain the fruit. Brush the pastry with the beaten egg and sprinkle with a little granulated sugar.

Put in the oven and bake for 25 minutes until golden. Allow the galettes to cool slightly before serving with a sifting of icing (confectioners') sugar and cream or ice cream.

COFFEE GRANITA

Granita is a traditional iced dessert served throughout Italy. I usually make it with decaffeinated coffee. If you can't get hold of decaffeinated espresso coffee, use twice as much standard grind instead.

Serves 4

40 g/1½ oz/½ cup ground espresso coffee

40 g/1½ oz/3 tbsp granulated sugar

½ tbsp lemon juice

2 tbsp icing (confectioners) sugar (optional)

In a pan, heat the ground coffee with 500 ml/18 fl oz/2 cups water. Bring to the boil, stir well and remove from the heat. Leave to stand for five minutes before straining through a coffee filter or muslin cloth. Add the sugar to the coffee and stir to dissolve. Add the lemon juice and leave to cool. Taste for sweetness – you want it to taste a bit too sweet as it will taste less sweet when frozen. Chill in the refrigerator.

Once chilled, decant into a large flat dish that will fit your freezer. You want the coffee mixture to be no deeper than 2 cm/¾ inch so that it freezers faster.

Freeze for 45 minutes. With a fork, break up any ice crystals that are forming around the edges. Repeat every 30–60 minutes until you have a fully crystalised texture throughout the mixture.

Serve the granita in glasses or small jars.

LEMON RICOTTA CAKE

Italian cakes tend to be dense and moist and packed full of delicate flavour, just like this one. This lemon and ricotta cake works equally well for dessert as it does for sharing with friends coming round for coffee.

Serves 10–12

125 g/4 ½ oz /½ cup/1 stick unsalted butter, softened

200 g/7 oz/1 cup granulated sugar

2½ tbsp lemon zest, about 4–5 lemons

3 large (extra-large) eggs

1 tsp vanilla extract

185 g/6½ oz 1½ cups plain (all-purpose) flour

2 tsp baking powder

¼ tsp salt

350 g/12 oz/1½ cups ricotta cheese

100 g/3½ oz flaked almonds

icing (confectioners') sugar for dredging

Preheat the oven to 180°C/350°F/Gas Mark 4. Butter a 23 cm/9 inch springform cake pan and line the base with baking parchment.

In a food processor or mixer, beat together the sugar, butter and lemon zest until pale and fluffy. With the processor on, mix in the eggs one at a time, as well as the vanilla.

Add in half of the flour, the baking powder and salt and process until just mixed. Add the ricotta and process until just mixed. Add in the rest of the flour until combined. Take care not to over-process the batter.

Pour the batter into the cake pan and spread out evenly. Scatter over the flaked almonds. Bake in the oven covered with baking parchment for 45–50 minutes until the cake is set and a knife pushed into its centre comes out clean.

Leave to cool for 10 minutes then run a knife around edge before removing the springform ring. Continue to cool, placing the pan base on a wire rack.

Once cool, dredge with icing (confectioners') sugar before serving.

INDEX

Entries with upper-case initials indicate recipes.

A

Apricot Tarte Tatin 206
aubergine 31
   Aubergine Cannelloni 137
   Baba Ganoush (Aubergine & Yogurt Dip) 82
   Griddled Aubergine (Eggplant) with Yogurt 96
   Moussaka 180
   Quick Ratatouille 140
   Roast Vegetable & Feta Salad 130
   Vegetable Tagine 148
Aubergine Cannelloni 137

B

Baba Ganoush (Aubergine & Yogurt Dip) 82
Baccalà alla Livornese 176
Baked Fish with Sun-Dried Tomatoes & Olives 152
Bouillabaisse 100
Breaded Pork with Panzanella 200

C

capers 27, 56
   Baccalà alla Livornese 176
   Chicken Piccata 194
   Pasta with Fresh Tomato Sauce 144
Cherry Tomato & Chicken Farfalle 190
Cherry Tomato & Mozzarella Salad 92
Chicken Chasseur 186
Chicken Feta Salad 124
Chicken Piccata 194
chickpea 50
   Hummus 84
   Moroccan Lamb with Apricots 188

Classic Greek Salad 126
Classic Grilled Fish 154
Classic Italian Tomato Sauce 88
Coffee Granita 218
courgette 32
   Courgette (Zucchini) Antipasti 94
   Quick Ratatouille 140
   Roast Vegetable & Feta Salad 130
   Simple Fish & Veg En Papillote 160
   Vegetable Tagine 148
Courgette (Zucchini) Antipasti 94

E

eggplant (see aubergine)

F

Figgy Yogurt Pots 78
fish and seafood 7, 8, 12, 15, 16, 18, 23, 36, 40, 42, 43, 44, 54, 60
   Baccalà alla Livornese 176
   Baked Fish with Sun-Dried Tomatoes & Olives 152
   Bouillabaisse 100
   Breaded Pork with Panzanella 200
   Classic Grilled Fish 154
   Griddled Aubergine (Eggplant) with Yogurt 96
   Mediterranean Chowder 116
   Mussels Linguine 168
   New Potato & Anchovy Salad 122
   Paella 171
   Parma-Ham-Wrapped Cod 166
   Potato Boulangère with Grilled Fish 164
   Prawn & Grapefruit Salad 120
   Quick Mediterranean Prawns 108
   Salade Niçoise 128
   Seafood Risotto 174
   Seafood Salad 156
   Seared Sea Bass on Tagliatelle 158
   Sicilian Sardine Pasta 162

Simple Fish & Veg En Papillote 160
Smoked Salmon Avocado Toasts 74
Taramasalata 86
Flourless Chocolate Orange Cake 204
French Onion Tart 132

G

garbanzo see chickpea
Goats' Cheese & Lemon Tart 211
Greek Yogurt with Honey-poached Nectarine 72
Griddled Aubergine (Eggplant) with Yogurt 96
Griddled Garlic & Lemon Squid 114
Griddled Peaches with Thyme & Honey 214

H

Halloumi & Smashed Avocado Sandwich 70
healthy fats 23, 24, 47
Herby Lamb & Yogurt Pitas 196
honey 50
   Greek Yogurt with Honey-poached Nectarine 72
   Griddled Peaches with Thyme & Honey 214
   Honey Baklava 208
   Oven-baked Chicken with Potato Wedges 192
Honey Baklava 208
Hummus 84

I

Italian Minestrone Soup 103

K

key foods 31

L

Labne with Peas & Arugula 76
Lemon Ricotta Cake 220

M

Mediterranean Chowder 116

Mediterranean Scrambled Eggs 68
Moroccan Lamb with Apricots 188
Moussaka 180
Mushroom Galette 134
Mussels Linguine 168

N
New Potato & Anchovy Salad 122

O
olive 27, 56
  Baked Fish with Sun-Dried
    Tomatoes & Olives 152
  Classic Greek Salad 126
  Classic Grilled Fish 154
  Pasta with Fresh Tomato
    Sauce 144
  Roast Vegetable & Feta
    Salad 130
  Salade Niçoise 128
  Spinach, Feta & Olive
    Parcels 112
  Stuffed Peppers 146
olive oil 12, 18, 23, 24, 50, 56
Oven-baked Chicken with Potato
  Wedges 192

P
Paella 171
Parma-Ham-Wrapped Cod 166
pasta 15, 32, 36, 39, 47, 54, 56
  Cherry Tomato & Chicken
    Farfalle 190
  Italian Minestrone Soup 103
  Mussels Linguine 168
  Pasta Primavera 142
  Pasta with Fresh Tomato
    Sauce 144
  Seared Sea Bass on
    Tagliatelle 158
  Sicilian Sardine Pasta 162
Pasta Primavera 142
Pasta with Fresh Tomato
  Sauce 144
Pork Shish Skewers 198
Potato Boulangère with Grilled
  Fish 164
Prawn & Grapefruit Salad 120

Q
Quick Mediterranean Prawns
  108
Quick Ratatouille 140

R
Roast Vegetable & Feta Salad
  130
Roasted Red Pepper, Tomato &
  Red Onion Soup 106
Roasted Tomato & Mozzarella
  Breakfast Bruschetta 66
Romesco Sauce 90

S
Salade Niçoise 128
Seafood Risotto 174
Seafood Salad 156
Seared Sea Bass on Tagliatelle
  158
Shakshuka 64
Sicilian Sardine Pasta 162
Simple Fish & Veg En Papillote
  160
Smoked Salmon Avocado Toasts
  74
Spicy Chicken Skewers with
  Mango Tabbouleh 183
Spinach & Green Bean Frittata
  110
Spinach, Feta & Olive Parcels
  112
Strawberry Galettes 216
Stuffed Peppers 146

T
Taramasalata 86
tomato 35, 54, 56
  Aubergine Cannelloni 137
  Baccalà alla Livornese 176
  Baked Fish with Sun-Dried
    Tomatoes & Olives 152
  Bouillabaisse 100
  Breaded Pork with Panzanella
    200
  Paella 171
  Cherry Tomato & Chicken
    Farfalle 190

Cherry Tomato & Mozzarella
  Salad 92
Chicken Chasseur 186
Chicken Feta Salad 124
Classic Greek Salad 126
Classic Grilled Fish 154
Classic Italian Tomato Sauce 88
Herby Lamb & Yogurt Pitas 196
Italian Minestrone Soup 103
Moroccan Lamb with
  Apricots 188
Moussaka 180
Mushroom Galette 134
Mussels Linguine 168
Pasta with Fresh Tomato
  Sauce 144
Roast Vegetable & Feta
  Salad 130
Roasted Red Pepper, Tomato &
  Red Onion Soup 106
Roasted Tomato & Mozzarella
  Breakfast Bruschetta 66
Romesco Sauce 90
Salade Niçoise 128
Seared Sea Bass on
  Tagliatelle 158
Shakshuka 64
Simple Fish & Veg En
  Papillote 160
Stuffed Peppers 146
Vegetable Tagine 148

V
Vegetable Tagine 148

W
wine 16, 24
  Baccalà alla Livornese 176
  Chicken Chasseur 186
  Chicken Piccata 194
  Mussels Linguine 168
  Seafood Risotto 174

Z
zucchini see courgette

If you enjoyed this book please sign up for updates,
information and offers on further titles in this series at
www.flametreepublishing.com